Collecting Bookmarkers

Books by the same author

Blue and White Transfer Ware 1780-1840
Blue-printed Earthenware 1800-1850
Buying Antiques Dictionary of Names
Historic English Inns

Collecting Bookmarkers

A. W. Coysh

Drake Publishers Inc New York

ISBN 0 7153 6722 6

LCCCN 74 13577

Printed in Great Britain

CONTENTS

ACKNOWLEDGEMENTS

Many people have helped me to assemble the collection of bookmarkers which forms the basis of this book. Some have been given to me, others lent to me, and many friends, officials, and booksellers have responded willingly to my requests for information. In particular I wish to thank Miss Jane Allport, Mr Basil Blackwell, Lady Brightman, Mr G. C. Browning, Mr M. R. Burman, Dr Peter Carter, Mrs Elizabeth Collard, Miss Kate Deas, Mr J. W. Gauler, Mr J. E. Gray, Mr S. B. Hamilton, Mr Gilbert Jamieson, Mr John Letts, Mrs Brenda Salmon and Mr John W. Waterer. I owe a special debt of gratitude to Mr Richard Clements who has been responsible for the illustrations.

A. W. Coysh

COLLECTING BOOKMARKERS

Most of the bookmarkers illustrated in this book are from a single collection made by the author over a relatively short period. They were acquired from second-hand bookshops, saleroom lots, received by post in response to advertisements in booksellers' journals, or given by friends. Bookmarkers provide a new field for the collector. There are many who collect other types of ephemera—bookplates, Christmas cards, matchbox labels, postcards, posters, tram tickets, trade cards and valentines—but there are few collectors of bookmarkers. So here is an opportunity for those of moderate means to assemble fascinating relics of Victorian and Edwardian days, as well as later examples, and at the same time to preserve them for posterity for they normally find their way into the waste-paper-basket or the bonfire. Young collectors can start with today's bookmarkers often issued free to borrowers from public libraries or given away as advertisements by booksellers.

The need for some device to mark the place in a book was recognised at an early date. Without bookmarkers finely bound volumes were at risk. To lay a book face down with pages open might cause injury to its spine, and the crease on a page that had had the corner turned down remained as a lasting reproach. Bookmarkers appear to have been used in Tudor times. In 1584 Queen Elizabeth was presented with a fringed silk bookmarker by Christopher Barker who had acquired a patent as Queen's Printer in 1577 which gave him the sole right to print the Bible, the Book of Common Prayer, the Statutes of the Realm and all proclamations. He was also a draper: hence the silk for the bookmarker. The British and Foreign Bible Society owns a bookmarker with plaited silk cords, silver knots and silk tassels which appears to have been made for use in a bible of 1632.

The common type of bookmarker in the eighteenth and early nineteenth centuries consisted of a narrow silk ribbon, seldom more than a centimetre in width, bound into the book at the top of the spine and just long enough to project below the lower edge of the page. These were quite common by about 1800 and many well-bound books were equipped in this way until World War I when their use declined. They are still used occasionally, however, especially in reference books.

The first detached and therefore collectable bookmarkers began to appear in the 1850s. One of the first references to these is found in Mary Russell Mitford's *Recollections of a Literary Life* (1852): 'I had no marker and the richly bound volume closed as if instinctively.' Buldeschi's *Ceremonial* (1853) gives the following instruction to the cleric in training: 'When carrying the Missal, he will take care not to displace the markers.' Note the abbreviation of 'bookmarker' to 'marker'. The modern abbreviation is usually 'bookmark'. For convenience both these forms will be used from time to time in this book.

Most nineteenth-century bookmarks were intended for use in bibles and prayer books and were made of ribbon. It was not until the 1880s that paper bookmarks became common. The history of bookmarks falls roughly into four main periods:

1850–1880 The Ribbon Period

Markers were often home-made from pieces of ribbon embroidered by hand or, more usually, to which an embroidered perforated card or small water-colour drawing was stitched. In the 1860s and 1870s woven silk bookmarks flooded the market. They were made by several firms in the Midlands of which Thomas Stevens of Coventry was the most important.

1880–1901 The Victorian Advertising Period

After about 1880 markers were printed on stiff paper or thin card. They usually carried advertisements, sometimes for a single product, sometimes for a range of products, especially soap, ladies corsets and garments, popular foods and quack medicines. Most of these advertisements were brash and insensitive.

1901–1914 The Pre-World War I Period

In Edwardian times advertising became more restrained and respectable. The insurance companies and publishers made great use of bookmarkers to interest the public in the services they provided. Brash advertising declined.

1914–Present Day Publicity and Greetings Period

Although some advertising continued on bookmarks

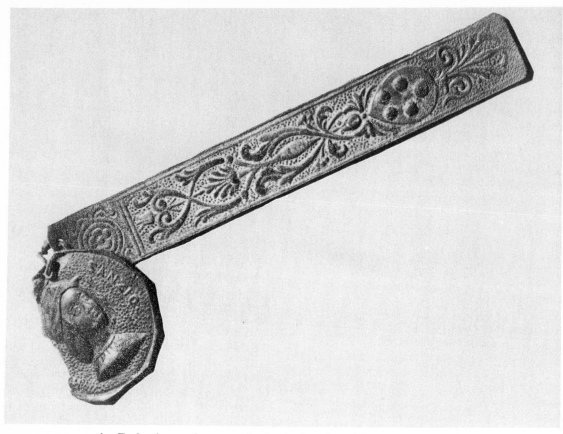

1   *Early nineteenth-century leather bookmarker of Italian origin, found
in an English leather-bound volume dated 1785.*

after World War I, much more use was made of
markers to carry publicity material and propaganda
for non-profit-making enterprises. They were used
to promote the war effort in both world wars, to
encourage people to save money, and to urge road
users to observe the Highway Code. Public libraries
used them, and still do today, to disseminate information. Private bodies used them for launching
appeals.

Some silk ribbons were still used after 1914,
especially for printed 'In Memoriam' markers, but
paper and card predominated. Occasionally new
synthetic materials such as celluloid were employed.
Traditional materials including silver and tortoise-
shell were designed to make more permanent
bookmarkers which could be carried in the pocket.

After World War II there was a revival of the
greetings bookmarker, especially the type which

would also serve as a Christmas card, sometimes
specially printed for the sender.

Today, bookmarkers carrying advertising material
are often attached to particular volumes, usually
reference books, by a strong silk cord. The object
is to reach the particular group of people the
advertiser is anxious to attract. Pharmaceutical
advertisements, for example, appear on a bookmark
attached to *The Hospitals Year Book* and makers
of civic plate will take space on a marker in *The
Municipal Year Book*. These are all worth adding
to a collection when the opportunity occurs; in a
few years they will begin to have the interest that
Victorian and Edwardian markers have for us today.

Starting a Collection

The pleasure of collecting bookmarkers, as with
other ephemera, is almost directly related to the

amount of research one is prepared to do. Each marker presents a series of problems. When was it made? What purpose did it serve in addition to the obvious one of marking a page in a book? Who made it and who was responsible for the design? It is seldom possible to answer all these questions but the attempt will lead to excursions into architecture, design, heraldry, history, typography and many other fields. Accurate information should be sought; speculation is dangerous.

The marker illustrated (1) was found in a leather-bound quarto volume of the sixth edition of *Johnson's Dictionary of the English Language* published in 1785. The leather of which it was made was hard and brittle, the colouring and gilt on the surface rubbed and worn. The head on the seal-like attachment gave the impression of age. Surely this must be an eighteenth-century bookmarker? However, it seemed wise to get an expert opinion and the Museum of Leathercraft in London suggested that Mr John W. Waterer might be asked to look at it. After examination he expressed the view that the marker was probably made of goatskin and the appended seal of sheepskin, both embossed with metal dies in a small press. The colouring and the gilding had probably been painted on by hand. The view was also expressed that the portrait on the seal is that of Raphael Sanzio who spent much of his working life in Florence. Taking into account the state of the leather, Mr Waterer came to the conclusion that the marker was probably made in Florence in the first half of the nineteenth century, or even after 1850, and that it may have been brought to England as a souvenir of the Italian city. However, the marker has considerable interest and is now in the Museum of Leathercraft. The lesson to be learned is that one must never assume that a bookmarker can be dated by noting the publication date of the book in which it is found.

One of the great advantages of collecting bookmarkers is that they are easy to store. They are seldom more than 20cm in length so a quarto loose-leaf file serves well for storage and display. The mount should be of white card or stiff paper and a page will normally serve for two, or sometimes three, markers. The paper or card bookmarks are easy to deal with. If a small diagonal slit is made for each corner in the mount the markers can be inserted much as postcards are in an old postcard album.

The mounting of silk markers needs a little more care. They should *never* be folded. Old silk tends to become brittle and is liable to split along the line of a fold. The best way to keep such markers in good condition is to protect them behind a layer of non-adhesive covering film. Cut out a piece a little larger than the marker, place it over the marker held against the mount, and seal the edges with sellotape. Before doing this be sure to note any interesting material woven on the reverse side—the name of the maker, the place of manufacture, and perhaps a registration mark. If for any reason the marker has to be removed from the mount at a later date it is better to cut away the covering completely before removing the silk. One of the advantages of the loose-leaf method of storage is that sheets of paper with notes can be inserted between the mounted pages. This will provide a layout not unlike the layout of this book. Moreover the order of the pages can be changed if it seems desirable to reclassify.

Do not hesitate to ask people to look out for bookmarkers for you. The author has been given at least half the markers seen in this book by friends, librarians or dealers. A dealer, however, should be offered payment. These are, after all, part of his stock in trade. Most paper markers can be secured for a few pence but good woven silk markers may cost several pounds. They are keenly collected, especially in America.

The following books will prove useful to the collector.

Browning, D. C. *Everyman's Dictionary of Literary Biography* (London, 1969)

Buday, G. *The History of the Christmas Card* (London, 1954. New ed 1964).

Darby, M. and Sprake, D. *Stevengraphs* (Guernsey, 1968)

De Vries, L. *Victorian Advertisements* (London, 1968)

De Vries, L. and Von Amstel, I. *The Wonderful World of American Advertisements* (London and New York, 1973)

Godden, G. A. *Stevengraphs and Other Victorian Silk Pictures* (London, 1971)

Hutchings, R. S. *A Manual of Decorative Type Faces* (London, 1965)

Litchen, F. *Decorative Art of Victoria's Era* (New York, 1950)

Norbury, J. *Victoriana* (London, 1972)

Staff, S. *The Valentine and its Origins* (London, 1969)

Sutphen, D. *The Old Mad Ads* (New York, 1960; London, 1968)

Wood, R. *Victorian Delights, Playbills, Posters and Ephemera of the Period* (London, 1967)

VICTORIAN CRAFT BOOKMARKERS

Embroidery

In early Victorian times coloured ribbon was widely used to decorate dresses and bonnets. The small unused bits could be made very conveniently into bookmarkers and these were often embroidered with silk thread. This parlour craft for women and especially for children continued the tradition of sampler embroidery. In the 1850s it was possible to buy sheets of strong perforated card which was far better than canvas for this type of embroidery because it did not stretch. Moreover, designs could be worked out in relation to the perforations which were set close together and were regularly spaced with about 500 to the square inch (nearly 80 per square centimetre). For a bookmarker a rectangular piece was cut a little narrower than the ribbon on which it would later be stitched.

The designs on these markers are mainly built around texts since they were made for the bibles and prayer books carried to church on Sundays and kept on the bedside table during the week. They invariably reflect the moral earnestness of the period. The following have been noted: 'Give and it shall be given unto you', 'Incline thine ear', 'The Bible our Guide', 'Let us with a gladsome mind praise the Lord for He is kind', 'Prayer', 'Search the Scriptures', and 'Turris Fortis Mihi Deus'. The examples illustrated (4 and 5) might equally have been embroidered in America or Britain for this type of craft was common to both countries. (See F. Litchen *Decorative Art of Victoria's Era*. New York, 1950)

Embroidered bookmarkers were sometimes made to give to a friend, relative, or sweetheart, and examples often bear the name of the recipient. Miss Randall (2) may have been a teacher or governess. The Reverend F. S. Keeling (3) was a minister in Liskeard, Cornwall. The author has a large marker of this type over 60cm in length, intended for a church or family bible, embroidered with the words 'Affections offering to F. M. Keeling, Liskeard, April 1870', possibly a gift to the minister's wife from a group of parishioners. This is a fairly late example of the craft which began to decline in the 1870s.

Occasionally the card was cut into a decorative shape (6) and beads were sometimes added despite the fact that they were clearly unsuitable for use between the pages of a book. One example has been noted in which the perforated paper was cut into

2 *Victorian blue silk-ribbon marker (c1870) with perforated card (9.1 × 3.3cm) embroidered with blue silk thread with the name 'Miss Randall'.*

3 *Victorian red silk-ribbon marker (c1870) with perforated card (12.4 × 2.3cm) embroidered with brown silk thread with the name 'Rev. F. S. Keeling'.*

4 *Victorian red silk-ribbon marker (c1860–70) with perforated card (13.7 × 3cm) embroidered with red silk thread with the words 'In God is our trust'.*

5 *Victorian red silk-ribbon marker (c1860–70) with perforated card (16.2 × 3.6cm) embroidered with red and yellow silk thread with a design reading 'The Holy [Book] our Chart'.*

6 *Victorian dark blue silk-ribbon marker (c1860–70) with perforated card (15.5 × 4.1cm) embroidered with dark blue silk thread with the words 'Forget me not'. The borders are decorated with threaded beads.*

Note: Only parts of the silk ribbons on which the perforated cards have been stitched have been shown. The full length of the ribbons varies from 25.4 to 30.5cm.

the shape of a crucifix and stitched on to black silk ribbon with no additional embroidery—obviously for use during a period of mourning.

Silk-ribbon bookmarkers with embroidered perforated card became so popular that card makers soon decided to produce special rectangular cards with decorative edges for use on the larger markers used in family bibles. When these were embroidered the themes were invariably religious. The example with the anchor (7) is typical. The ribbon has a black edge which made it suitable for use during a period of mourning and the anchor as a symbol of hope was also appropriate. Indeed, the anchor is frequently seen on mourning jewellery, often associated with a cross and a heart to represent faith, hope and charity.

These decorative cards were sometimes used as mounts for small pictures or for photographs. The example (9) has a picture which illustrates the theme of the embroidery. When photographs were used they were usually of a well-known religious picture of the crucifixion or of Christ wearing the crown of thorns.

The break from purely religious subjects came in the 1880s when small coloured Christmas cards were occasionally stitched to silk markers. Some Christmas cards were actually printed on long narrow strips and it may be that the makers had this use in mind. (See G. Buday *The History of the Christmas Card*. 1964. Colour plates X, XIa and c)

The embroidered bookmarkers used by the clergy in churches were much more elaborate in Victorian times. They were changed with the pulpit fall and draperies according to the season or festival in the church year, a practice which continues in many churches today. Markers of white, cream and gold were used for joyful occasions such as Christmas and Ascensiontide, and sometimes on saint's days. Purple symbolized penance and preparation and was used during Lent. Green was not attached to any special event in the calendar but as nature's colour signified God's provision for our welfare. Red, signifying fire and blood, was appropriate for martyr's days.

7 *Victorian peach-coloured silk-ribbon marker (c1865–70) with corded black edge. Decorative perforated card (15.7 × 6.1cm) which is stitched to the ribbon is embroidered in brown, green, red and black silk with an anchor entwined with leaves and flowers.*

8 *Victorian dark maroon silk-ribbon marker (c1870–80) on which a small Christmas card (7.7 × 4.8cm) has been stitched by the corners.*

9 *Victorian dark blue silk-ribbon marker (c1870–80) with decorative perforated card (17.3 × 6.6cm) embroidered with the words 'Feed My Lambs' below a coloured print pasted on the card.*

Hope
is the
of the
soul

Pussy and I have brought these flowers

And wish you merry Christmas hours.

FEED
MY
LAMBS.

Hand-painted Bookmarkers

Drawing and painting were as important as embroidery as domestic crafts in Victorian times and many amateurs reached a high standard. The way had been prepared early in the nineteenth century when there was tremendous interest in water-colour painting in professional circles. The Society of Painters in Water Colours was founded in 1805 and later became known as the 'Old Society' when The New Society of Painters in Miniature and Water-colours came into being in 1807. The following year saw the formation of The Associated Artists in Water-colours and in 1831 the Royal Institute of Painters in Water-colours was established. Interest soon spread to amateur circles. Painting in water-colours was cleaner and more convenient than in oils on canvas. It was more ladylike. In Victorian times upper and middle class ladies and their children were constantly drawing and painting. When a Victorian house with its contemporary furnishings and effects is sold there is almost always a folder of such amateur work in the saleroom.

It is not surprising to find that many bookmarkers were hand-painted. The religious marker (11) has a beautifully executed water-colour drawing stitched to the ribbon, well up to professional standards. The other three painted markers (10, 12 and 13), however, show the hand of the amateur. Two of these (10 and 13) were found in books of the 1860–70 period and although it is not always wise to try to date bookmarkers by the period of the books in which they are found it seems likely in these cases that they may have remained in books of their period. The greetings marker (12) is almost certainly much later.

Cut Paper Bookmarkers

These occasionally turn up in old books and give the impression of lace against a dark background. The skills used were those of the silhouettist except that the cut-out was made from white paper placed against a dark-coloured ribbon whereas the silhouettist used black paper against a white ground. A knife was used for cutting rather than scissors and the paper was stitched or stuck to the ribbon to make the bookmarker. A good example is illustrated in J. Norbury's *Victoriana* (1972), plate 14.

10 *Victorian marker (c1860–70) painted in water-colours on thin cream card. The design includes the words:*

 'Who shuts his hand hath lost his Gold
 Who opens it hath it twice told.'

Length 19.5cm.

11 *Victorian marker (c1860–70) painted in water-colours on cream paper backed by stiff card with a wooden cross, a spray of corn chamomile and a ribbon with the words: 'I will never leave thee, nor forsake thee'. The card is sewn with long stitches to a red silk ribbon. Length of card 15.7cm. The ribbon has been torn so that it does not extend to its original length.*

12 *Late Victorian or Edwardian marker (c1895–1910) painted in water-colours on stiff white card. Length 19.8cm.*

13 *Victorian marker (c1860–70) painted in water-colours and gilt on stiff card. Length 19.8cm.*

Who shuts his hand hath lost his Gold
Who opens it hath it twice told.

11　　　**12**　　　**13**

Will never leave thee, nor forsake thee.

BEST WISHES

WOVEN SILK BOOKMARKERS

The weaving of silk ribbon was an established industry in Coventry in the early part of the eighteenth century and flourished until the middle of the nineteenth century, employing nearly half the labour force of the city. In 1851 the ribbon manufacturers and the townsfolk co-operated to produce a special ribbon for the Great Exhibition which later became known as the 'Coventry Ribbon'. It was designed by Thomas Clack, a pupil at the Coventry School of Design, and was drafted for the Jacquard loom by Robert Barton, the cost being covered by public subscription. The drafting process involved enlarging the original design and showing each thread in the colour to be used. From this draft the cards were prepared for the machine, the coloured threads passing through hundreds of perforations in the cards. Drafting was therefore a key process combining artistry with technical knowledge.

The Coventry industry had long been protected from competition by an import tax on ribbon. In 1860 this tax was lifted and fine ribbon from France flowed into the country duty free. At the same time fashions were changing. The bonnet decorated with ribbon was slowly being replaced by the hat decorated with feathers. As a result there was a slump in the ribbon trade which hit the Coventry manufacturers particularly hard. Some attempt was made to find alternative work for the weavers but many left the city and whole families emigrated.

The success of the Coventry Ribbon, however, had encouraged several manufacturers to attempt to weave decorative ribbons on the Jacquard loom. In 1861 the firm of Dalton, Barton & Co Ltd exhibited a ribbon in the Coventry Drapers' Hall of 'England's Royal Sailor, Highness Prince Alfred Ernest Albert'. When the Prince Consort died in December of that year a number of firms produced woven ribbons with his portrait. The ribbon by J. & J. Cash (14) was one of the earliest. It was designed and drafted by the men who had been responsible for the Coventry Ribbon, and was available early in 1862. *The Coventry Herald and Observer* for March 28 of that year describes it as 'certainly the best ribbon of this class we have yet seen ... not so much for the likeness of the Prince ... but rather for its accessories of Rosenau, the birthplace of Prince Albert, and of Windsor where he died, which are exquisitely done, each making a pretty little picture as if it were in the best style of engraving'. It is not clear whether this ribbon was

14 *Silk ribbon (1862) woven in black and white by J. & J. Cash of Coventry to commemorate the death of HRH the late Prince Consort in 1861. The portrait is surmounted by a view of Rosenau, his birthplace, and below is a view of Windsor where he died. The manufacturer's name is woven in the silk at the base of the ribbon which is still attached to the card on which it was sold. Length of ribbon 25.9cm.*

15 *Silk bookmarker (c1868–70) woven in black, green, purple, red and yellow by Thomas Stevens with a design in the Gothick style listed in his advertisements as 'Have mercy upon us', Charity Girls. Length 38.8cm. The reverse side shows the maker's name: 'T. Stevens Coventry'.*

16 *Silk bookmarker (1871) woven by Thomas Stevens in brown, blue, green, purple, red and yellow with Eliza Cook's poem 'The Old Arm Chair' and the music score for the first verse. The title of the poem has below it a picture of the chair on which rests a bible. Length 25.7cm. The reverse side has the maker's name: 'T. Stevens Coventry' and a diamond-shaped registration mark for 4 May 1871.*

15

H.R.H. PRINCE CONSORT.

BORN AT ROSENAU. AUG. 26. 1819.
DIED AT WINDSOR DEC. 14. 1861.

J. J. Cash Coventry

16

intended for use as a bookmarker but it was certainly used for this purpose: the example illustrated came from a large book of the period.

Very soon bookmarkers woven in colour were being advertised. These were folded back at the base to form a point to which a coloured silk tassel was attached. Thomas Stevens of Coventry soon became pre-eminent in the field and by October 1862 was offering over fifty different designs, mainly with religious themes, though one or two carried Christmas or birthday greetings. By 1870 he had added over a hundred new designs. The larger markers such as the 'Charity Girls' sold for 1s 6d each. Some examples bear a woven mark to indicate when the design was registered. 'The Old Arm Chair' (16), for example, bears the mark for 4 May 1871. The poem by Eliza Cook first appeared in the *Weekly Dispatch* in 1836 when the poetess was only eighteen years of age. She was still writing in the 1870s when this marker was issued. Eliza Cook was born in Southwark, the youngest of a brassworker's eleven children, and was self-educated. Although she published several volumes of poetry and edited a paper called *Eliza Cook's Journal* from 1849 to 1854, *The Old Arm Chair* remained her best-known work.

Although religious and devotional markers predominated in the early days, those with a greeting or message soon appeared in increasing numbers and flooded the market by the 1870s. The 'Many Happy Returns of the Day' example (17) was registered by Thomas Stevens in 1874. Many of these markers are decorated with flowers which were symbolic of human emotions. In the language of flowers the poppy on a black ground (17) is for consolation, to be sent to someone who has lost a loved one. The convolvulus on the 'Remember Me' marker (18) stands for extinguished hopes, and the forget-me-not and chrysanthemum on the 'Your Birthday' marker (19) both stand for true love. Indeed, it would be possible to make a collection of markers reflecting the whole language of flowers which was so significant in Victorian times.

The 'Your Birthday' marker (19) is of particular interest because it carries the name of Edward Bollans & Co of Leamington. This firm, described as 'wholesale manufacturers of fancy stationery', appears to have been in business from about 1863 at 14 Ranelagh Terrace, Leamington. They registered the design for a woven silk bookmarker in 1870; by 1872 there were forty-nine on their list and by 1873 over eighty. A list of Bollans's markers is given in G. A. Godden's *Stevengraphs and Other*

17 *Silk bookmarker (1874) woven in black, green, purple, red and yellow by Thomas Stevens with a birthday message. The marker has its original red silk tassel. Length (without tassel) 20.5cm.*
The reverse side has the woven mark: 'T. Stevens Coventry' and a diamond-shaped registration mark for 28 February 1874.

18 *Silk bookmarker (1870s) woven in green, purple, red and yellow by Thomas Stevens with a 'Remember Me' message. Length 15.3cm.*
The reverse side has the woven mark: 'T. Stevens Coventry'.

19 *Silk bookmarker (c1873) woven in blue, green, red and yellow with a birthday message. Length 19.7cm.*
The reverse side has the woven mark on the top hem: 'E. Bollans & Co. Leamington'.

20 *Small silk bookmarker (c1900) woven in black, red and orange with a text from Exodus 33.14: 'M Presence shall go with Thee'. The marker has a white tassel. Length (without tassel) 9.6cm.*
The reverse side has the woven mark on the top hem: 'Marshall, Morgan & Scott Ltd. London'.

21 *Small silk bookmarker (c1900) woven in green, orange and pink with an anchor and a text from Psalms 48.14: 'He will be our Guide'. The marker has an orange tassel. Length (without tassel) 9.3cm. The reverse side has the woven mark: 'G.J.C (London)' on the lower hem and 'Made in England on the top hem.*

17

MANY HAPPY
RETURNS
OF THE
DAY

MANY HAPPY RETURNS
OF THE DAY OF THY BIRTH,
WITH HEALTH
AND PROSPERITY
PLEASURE AND MIRTH;
WITH HAPPINESS EVER;
BUT OH! MAY'ST THOU BE
AMID THY JOYS, NEVER
FORGETFUL OF ME.

18

Remember
Me

'TIS SWEET TO
BE REMEMBERED,
AS THROUGH THIS
WORLD WE STRAY;

TO KNOW WE HAVE
ONE KINDRED SOUL
TO CHEER US
ON OUR WAY.

19

YOUR
BIRTHDAY

FORGET ME NOT
ON THIS SWEET DAY,
WHEN FRIENDS ARE
PRESSING ROUND TO SAY
ALL KIND OF HEARTFELT
WISHES PURE,
THAT HAPPY HOURS MAY
LONG ENDURE.

20

MY
Presence
Shall
Go with
Thee
EX. 33. 14.

21

He
will be
our
Guide
Psa. 48:14.

Victorian Silk Pictures (1971), pp 408–9. According to directories Edward Bollans & Co continued in business until 1893 but in their final years were no longer described as 'manufacturers'. We do not know whether the firm actually had a loom to weave their own silks. It seems more likely that the woven markers were obtained from one of the Coventry makers, possibly from Welch & Lenton who not only designed for other firms but also made bookmarkers bearing their own name (24).

Two small markers (20 and 21) with the woven marks of London firms present a similar problem. They would both appear to be of a later date. Were they woven on small looms in London or made for these firms by a Coventry manufacturer?

After the death of the Prince Consort in 1861 when Queen Victoria observed her period of deep mourning for over twenty-five years, mourning after any death in a family was regarded as natural. Black dresses were worn, jet jewellery was the only adornment and even the bookmarker in the prayer book carried to church had to reflect the sad event. Black bookmarkers were common by the 1870s though the woven designs do not always reflect the mourning theme; the black grounds were a concession to convention. The Stevens marker (22) could well have been given as a valentine during a period of mourning. A hand holding a spray of flowers is certainly symbolic of mourning but the words express a different sentiment. The heart was a symbol of love and affection, and the shamrock in the language of flowers stood for light-heartedness. The Welch & Lenton marker (24), however, is a true mourning example.

The firm of Welch & Lenton operated at 1 Bailey Lane, Coventry from 1845 until early in the 1900s. The partnership was able to cope with every stage of production. Francis Welch and James Lenton were both designers, and Francis was also a draftsman. A few designs were registered in the firm's name, the first in 1862, but the bulk of their work was to design and draft for other makers, including Thomas Stevens. They had a considerable reputation in the trade and produced work of high quality. In 1874 a Welch & Lenton design was registered for a Miners' Union bookmarker which carried the words: 'God Bless the British Miner, what would the Country do without him?'

The 'In Memoriam' bookmarker (23) with the portrait of Queen Victoria was one of the last silk bookmarkers to be woven. The maker is unknown but it may well have been produced by W. H. Grant & Co of Foleshill, Coventry who within a few

22 *Silk bookmarker (1874) woven by Thomas Stevens in green, mauve, red and yellow on a black ground with a design 'To One I Love'. The marker has a yellow tassel. The word 'Copyright' appears below the hand and heart symbols. Length (without tassel) 16.4cm.*
The reverse side has the woven mark: 'T. Stevens Coventry' and a diamond-shaped registration mark for 2 December 1874.

23 *'In Memoriam' silk bookmarker (1901) with a portrait of Queen Victoria woven in black on a grey ground. Length 12cm.*

24 *Silk bookmarker (c1877–80) woven by Welch & Lenton in green, mauve, pink, white and yellow on a black ground. Length 18.5cm.*
The reverse side has the woven mark: 'Welch & Lenton Coventry'.

22

TO ONE
I LOVE

MY

AND

I OFFER
THEE
OH LET OUR

UNITED
BE

COPYRIGHT

23

In Memoriam
Queen Victoria

BORN MAY 24, DIED JAN 22
1819 ~ 1901
IN THE 64TH YEAR OF HER REIGN.

"AND THEY BURIED HER.
AND THE KING LIFTED UP HIS VOICE
AND WEPT AT THE GRAVE;
AND ALL THE PEOPLE WEPT.

AND THE KING SAID UNTO HIS
SERVANTS,   KNOW YE NOT
THAT THERE IS A PRINCE AND
A GREAT ONE FALLEN THIS DAY
IN ISRAEL."

24

GOOD
WISHES

O! MAY YOUR PATH
BE FULL OF
LIGHT,
OF PLEASING SIGHTS
AND SOUNDS,
AND WHERE 'MIDST
JOYS OF FAITHFUL
FRIENDS,
THE PEACE OF
GOD ABOUNDS.

weeks of the Queen's death registered designs for woven portraits of King Edward VII and Queen Alexandra.

Two classes of woven silk bookmarkers are of very special interest: those with portraits of famous people and those which were woven at various trade exhibitions. At these exhibitions Thomas Stevens would set up a loom and sell ribbons as souvenirs immediately they were woven. Sometimes there was not even time to finish them off with a tassel as was common with silk markers. A loom similar to those used at exhibitions has been set up in the Herbert Art Gallery and Museum at Coventry where bookmarkers can be woven for visitors.

Collectors may find markers from the following exhibitions:

1865 The International Exhibition, Dublin, opened by HRH Prince of Wales. (Thomas Stevens)

1866 Yorkshire Fine Art and Industrial Exhibition. (Thomas Stevens)

1867 Coventry and Midland Manufacturing, Industrial and Art Exhibition (25). This marker is said to have required 5,500 cards to form the pattern. It carries a portrait of Lord Leigh, the President, and a view of Stoneleigh Abbey where the exhibition was held. (Thomas Stevens)

1868 Crystal Palace Exhibition, Sydenham, London. The marker carries a portrait of Sir Joseph Paxton, the designer and architect of the building. (Thomas Stevens). (See G. A. Godden *Stevengraphs and Other Victorian Silk Pictures*. 1971. Plate 271.)

1869 South Staffordshire Industrial and Fine Art Exhibition, Wolverhampton. (Thomas Stevens)

1876 Centennial Exposition, Philadelphia, USA. The marker carries a portrait of George Washington (27). (Thomas Stevens)

1879 Yorkshire Fine Art and Industrial Exhibition. This was the occasion when Thomas Stevens first introduced his famous Stevengraph mounted pictures to the public. The exclusive right to make bookmarkers at the exhibition was granted to Welch & Lenton.

1893 World's Fair Columbia Exposition, Chicago, USA. Bookmarkers were made as souvenirs for this occasion not only by Thomas Stevens but also by W. H. Grant of Foleshill, Coventry. (See G. A. Godden, ibid, plate 291.)

Among the people illustrated on the portrait bookmarkers are: Captain HRH Alfred, Duke of Edinburgh; Hugh Bourne, Founder of the Primitive Methodists; Rt Hon John Bright; John Bunyan; Robert Burns (26); Captain Cook; Charles Dickens;

25 Silk bookmarker (1867) woven by Thomas Stevens in black, blue, green, red and yellow as a souvenir of the Coventry and Midland Manufacturing, Industrial and Art Exhibition held at Stoneleigh Abbey in June 1867. Length 35cm.
Note: This ribbon appears to have been sold just as it came from the loom without any attempt having been made to finish it off as a bookmarker.

26 Silk bookmarker (c1862) woven by Thomas Stevens in black and olive-green with a portrait of Robert Burns within a thistle wreath, and a view of his birthplace at Alloway, near Ayr. Length 17.6cm.
The reverse side has the woven mark: 'T. Stevens Coventry'.

27 Silk bookmarker (1876) woven by Thomas Stevens in blue, red, and yellow with a portrait of George Washington for the Centennial Exposition, Philadelphia, 1876. Length 22.4cm. The marker is still on the original card on which it was sold.

ICH DIEN

Coventry
and Midland
Manufacturing Industrial
and Art Exhibition
Opened June 1867

The Rt Hon Lord Leigh
President

STONELEIGH ABBEY

Should auld aquaintance be forgot,
And never brought to min'?
Should auld aquaintance be forgot,
And the days o' lang syne?

Robert Burns

SIX HIGHEST PRIZE MEDALS & DIPLOMA AWARDED TO

THOMAS STEVENS
COVENTRY & LONDON
INVENTOR AND MANUFACTURER
— OF THE —
PURE SILK WOVEN
BOOK MARKERS.
400 DIFFERENT DESIGNS.

1776   1876
CENTENNIAL
U.S.A.
THE FATHER OF OUR COUNTRY

GEORGE WASHINGTON.

The first in peace,
The first in war,
The first in the
Hearts of his
Countrymen.

PHILADELPHIA
1876.

Rt Hon Benjamin Disraeli; Garibaldi; Rt Hon W. E. Gladstone; General Grant; Dr Guthrie, apostle of the 'Ragged Schools'; Admiral Sir James Hope; 'Stonewall' Jackson; John Angell James, founder of Evangelical Alliance; John Knox, the Scottish divine; President Lincoln; Sir Joseph Paxton; J. G. Pike, a prominent baptist; Pope Pius IX; Robert Raikes, founder of Sunday schools; Sir Walter Scott; William Shakespeare; Charles Spurgeon, Calvinist preacher; HRH Prince of Wales; HRH Princess of Wales; Queen Victoria; George Washington; Cardinal Wiseman. This forms an interesting list of people who were in the public eye and the public mind in the thirty years between 1862 and 1893.

Woven silk bookmarkers were made on the Continent as well as in Britain. Two examples shown here (28 and 29) were produced as souvenirs for visitors to Alpine resorts. The Ötztaler Alpen are in the Austrian Tirol between the Inn valley and the Italian border, where the highest peak, Wild Spitz, rises to over 12,000ft. Saanenmöser is some twenty miles east of Montreux, on the watershed between the Sarine and the Simme rivers, and a skiing centre. It is difficult to date these markers but it seems likely that they were made by one of the two silk factories at Basle which were already weaving bookmarkers in the 1860s when Koechlin & Sons produced a portrait silk of Prince Albert, and Wahl & Socin a portrait of Queen Victoria. Both firms used the same designer —J. Bauman.

The marker from Holland (30) may have been a 'give-away' advertisement for a wine merchant. The saying 'Goede wijn behoeft geen krans' is the equivalent of 'Good wine needs no bush' derived from the epilogue of Shakespeare's As You Like It: 'If it be true that "good wine needs no bush", 'tis true that a good play needs no epilogue; yet to good wine they do use good bushes; and good plays prove the better by the help of good epilogues.'

This marker could well have been woven at St Etienne or Lyons, both famed for this kind of woven silk.

28 Silk bookmarker (date unknown) woven in black, blue and red on a white ground with a panel showing an Alpine scene. The locality is given as 'Ötztal Tirol in Austria. Length 16.2cm.

29 Christmas greetings silk bookmarker (date unknown) woven in black on a white ground for the Sporthotel Saanenmöser, Switzerland. Above and below an Alpine view there is a band of berried holly woven in green and red. Length 16.2cm.

30 Blue silk bookmarker (date unknown) woven in brown and silver with a bunch of grapes and a woman with basket. Between these decorations are the Dutch words: 'Goede wijn behoeft geen krans'. Length 15cm.

SPORTHOTEL SAANENMÖSER

MERRY CHRISTMAS & HAPPY NEWYEAR

Ötztal/Tirol

Goede wijn behoeft geen krans

PRINTED RIBBON BOOKMARKERS

Most woven silk bookmarkers were made in the 1870s. By the end of this decade Thomas Stevens was occupied with preparations to launch his mounted Stevengraph pictures. His last registered bookmarker design in 1880 was clearly a special order to mark the centenary of the first Sunday school opened by Robert Raikes in 1780. No doubt bookmarkers were still woven using the old designs but firms were turning more and more to the production of woven pictures and portraits. William Grant who learned his trade from Stevens and started on his own in 1880 produced relatively few bookmarkers though he did weave a souvenir marker for the Chicago Exhibition of 1893.

In the 1880s experiments were already being made with printing on silk. The Artistic Stationery Company issued a printed silk picture dated 1882 with a design by George Cruikshank entitled 'Our Times' (see G. A. Godden, *Stevengraphs and Other Victorian Silk Pictures*. 1971. Plate 309). Printed silk bookmarkers were also produced at about this period. One example has the text from Psalms: 'Thy word is a light unto my path' printed in silver on red silk. Another has a 'Motto' (31) adapted from the words of Stephen Grellet (1773–1855). The original version runs: 'I expect to pass through this world but once. Any good therefore that I can do, or any kindness I can show to any fellow creature, let me do it now. Let me not defer it or neglect it, for I shall not pass this way again.'

Note that 'fellow creature' has become 'human being, or dumb animal'. This reflects the sentimental attitude to the animal kingdom in late Victorian days when the works of Sir Edwin Henry Landseer had gained widespread popularity.

The marker in memory of King Edward VII (32) is poorly printed on a cheap cotton cloth and has been trimmed unevenly. These little markers may well have been mass-produced by printing on large pieces of cloth which were then cut up by hand.

At the end of World War I silk markers were being printed with 'In Memoriam' notices. The example shown here (33) is from Stockport. The author has another from Swindon which uses a different type-face and is decorated with an ivy leaf motif. This is dated 1923. It seems probable that these markers were printed locally on silk ribbon which the printer could buy.

31 Mauve silk bookmarker (c1890–1900) printed in black with a motto. Length 19cm.

32 White cotton bookmarker (1910) printed in black in memory of King Edward VII who died on 6 May 1910. The portrait is enclosed in a wreath of oak leaves, roses, shamrock and thistles and is surmounted by a view of Windsor Castle. Length 13.5cm.

33 White silk bookmarker (1918) printed in black with an 'In Memoriam' notice of a lady who died during the last year of World War I. Length with fringes 20cm.

32

MOTTO.

"I SHALL PASS
THROUGH THIS
WORLD BUT ONCE;
ANY GOOD THING
THEREFORE THAT I
CAN DO, OR ANY
KINDNESS THAT I
CAN SHOW TO ANY
HUMAN BEING, OR
DUMB ANIMAL,
LET ME DO IT
NOW; LET ME NOT
DEFER IT, OR
NEGLECT IT; FOR I
SHALL NOT PASS
THIS WAY AGAIN."

IN LOVING MEMORY
OF OUR
BELOVED KING

1901 1910

E.R

In loving remembrance of

Eliza Emma Livesley,

Who entered into rest

April 29th, 1918,

In her 73rd Year;

Interred Stockport Borough

Cemetery, May 2nd, 1918.

▫

Life's race well run,
Life's work well done,
Life's crown well won;
Now comes rest.

"She hath done what she could."

"Peace, perfect peace."

▫

63 Great Portwood Street,
Stockport.

RELIGIOUS BOOKMARKERS ON CARD

The religious bookmarkers which predominated in mid-Victorian times on embroidered or woven silk virtually disappeared before the end of the century. They were gradually replaced by religious markers on thin card after about 1880. Religious Christmas cards had been produced much earlier with designs based on paintings by well-known artists, but these had already begun to lose their popularity (see G. Buday *The History of the Christmas Card*. 1964, p 187). However, bookmarkers were different; they were largely for use in bibles and prayer books and a religious theme was appropriate. Some were printed with texts (34); others with nativity scenes (35 and 36) or hymn verses (37). Many were published by firms of church furnishers such as Mowbrays who still have premises in London and Oxford. The founder of the firm was Alfred Richard Mowbray who started the business in 1858 for the publication of tracts. It has always been accepted that Mowbrays were the first publishers of religious greetings cards. They issued many bookmarkers but ceased publishing late in the 1960s. The Mowbray marker (35) has a semicircular flap cut to fit over the edge of a page. The 'page-flap' became quite common in paper and card bookmarkers, especially in Edwardian times.

It is very difficult to date many of these religious markers. Catalogues were not common; specimens were usually carried round to retailers in a traveller's sample book. These were bulky items which soon became tattered as cards that had gone out of print were torn from the pages. Few have survived. In any case they were not reliable guides since many firms revived old patterns and reissued them in a slightly different form some years later.

The marker with the stained-glass window design (36) has the name of the designer, William Glasby, at the base of the window, though it is difficult to see. Such markers were from a larger drawing or watercolour, reduced in size, so a good magnifying glass is an essential piece of equipment for the bookmarker collector.

34 Religious bookmarker (c1880–1900) printed on t card in brown and red on a greenish-blue ground. T text is from Psalms XII.6. Length 16.3cm.
The reverse side is plain.

35 Religious bookmarker (c1900) printed in colour thin card with a nativity scene. The lettering is in and there is a semicircular page-flap. Length 14.2 The reverse side has the printed mark:

Mowbrays
Printed in England
1308

36 Religious bookmarker (1925) printed in colour thin card with a stained-glass window design of nativity signed by William Glasby and mar 'British'. Below the window a panel bears a and Christmas greeting. Length 16.6cm.
The reverse side has a handwritten greeting da 'Christmas 1925'.

37 Religious bookmarker (1920s) printed in colour thin card with a devotional scene. Below are verses of Augustus Toplady's hymn 'Rock of Ag A cord is attached so that the marker may be tied gift. Length 15.3cm.
The reverse side is plain.

35 **36** **37**

From East to West,
From shore to shore,
Let every heart
Awake and sing,
The Holy Child,
Whom Mary bore,
The Christ, the
Everlasting King.

"Behold I bring you Good
Tidings of Great Joy."
WITH BEST WISHES
FOR A VERY HAPPY
CHRISTMAS.

SIMPLY TO THY CROSS I CLING —

Rock of Ages,
    cleft for me,
Let me hide
    myself in Thee;
Let the water
    and the blood
From Thy riven
    side which flowed,
Be of sin the
    double cure,
Cleanse me from
    its guilt and power.

Nothing in my
    hand I bring;
Simply to Thy
    Cross I cling;
Naked, come to
    Thee for dress;
Helpless, look to
    Thee for grace;
Foul, I to the
    fountain fly;
Wash me, Saviour,
    or I die.

Made in
Great Britain.

COMMERCIAL BOOKMARKERS

Among the first commercial firms to advertise on bookmarkers was Brown & Polson. The Thackeray example (38) is very restrained compared with most Victorian advertisements. This has a calendar for 1884 and the second example (40) has a calendar for 1893 so it seems that the firm used this method of advertising over a considerable period. The change in style is interesting. The years from 1887 to 1893 saw the publication of the popular Kate Greenaway Almanacks decorated with figures of young children wearing beribboned bonnets. This artist had a considerable influence on commercial styles. The Brown & Polson girl (40) is certainly plumper than most of the Greenaway children but perhaps this is not inappropriate in view of her obviously large calorie intake. This marker has the name 'Ben George' in the lower left hand corner, an artist or printer as yet untraced.

When Brown & Polson advertised in *Sylvia's Journal* in 1878 they claimed twenty years' experience in the trade, so one must assume they were making cornflour in 1858. It was claimed to possess 'all the properties of the finest arrowroot' which was at that time extensively used as an ingredient in biscuits, blancmange and sauces.

In the 1890s *Mrs Beeton's Household Cookery* listed the following ingredients for a quart mould of blancmange: 1 pint new milk, 1¼oz isinglass, the rind of ½ lemon, ¼lb loaf sugar, 10 bitter almonds, and 1 pint of cream.

The cost was 3s, a considerable sum in those days. Cornflour was only mentioned in a footnote: 'A blancmange for children may be made from Brown & Polson's Corn-flour.'

It seems probable that the Brown & Polson bookmarkers were enclosed in the cornflour packets.

Day & Son of Berners Street, London, published bookmarkers with general advertising. These all had a silhouette of the London skyline with the dome of St Paul's Cathedral. Below this advertisements appeared on a panel representing a poster on a wall (39). Mellin's Food for children was widely advertised in many publications, especially those for women such as *Sylvia's Journal*. Bryant & May's trade mark depicting the Ark with the word 'Security' printed on it became very well known. It appeared on their 'all-round-the-box' labels, some of which also carried a shipping label, for their boxes of matches were given away by certain shipping companies to the passengers on their vessels.

38 Brown & Polson bookmarker (1884) printed black, grey and red on thin card with a portrait William Makepeace Thackeray. Length 18.7cm. The reverse side has a calendar for 1884 and the sta ment: 'Brown & Polson Corn Flour distinguis for uniformly superior quality.'

39 Day & Son bookmarker (c1890–1900) printed black on thin blue card with general advertising. Pa flap. Length 16.5cm. The reverse side is shown on page 33(43).

40 Brown & Polson bookmarker (1893) printed blue, brown, green, pink and black on thin card with advertisement for blancmange. Length 19.8cm. The reverse side has a calendar for 1893 and the sta ment: 'Brown & Polson's Corn-Flour has the long history and highest reputation.'

BROWN & POLSON'S

PORTRAIT
BOOK-MARK.

W.M. THACKERAY
BORN AT
CALCUTTA,
12TH AUGUST, 1811.
DIED IN
LONDON
Nr KENSINGTON PALACE
24TH DECR 1863.

BOOK-MARK

MELLIN'S FOOD
FOR
INFANTS
AND
INVALIDS
—
MELLIN'S
FOOD
BISCUITS.
Nourishing,
Palatable, Digestive
Sustaining,
2/0 & 3/6 PER TIN.

G. MELLIN,
Marlboro' Works,
Peckham, LONDON

Master BRADLEY, aged 18 Months,
"Brought up on Mellin's Food"

ASPINALL'S ENAMEL.
SUPPORT HOME INDUSTRIES.
BRYANT & MAY'S

SECURITY

TRADE MARK

Nineteen
Prize
Medals
MATCHES
For
Excellence
of Quality

THIS IS THE PAIR

HOVEN'S CLIP

HEALTH

BREESE LONDON

There is nothing better
than
'La Brillantine'
METALLIC POWDER.
As used by the Metropolitan
Fire Brigade, Household
Regiments, etc.
Boxes, 6d. & 1s. Post free.
Proprietors
J.F. BAUMGARTNER
& Co.,
15 B.M.), Newman Street,
Oxford Sts. London, W.

FOR
POLISHING
METALS,
Especially
BRASS.

DAY & SON BERNERS ST LONDON N.W.

Book
Mark

Brown & Polson's
Corn Flour.

The Day & Son bookmarker with the portrait of Mr C. B. Harness (41) is of particular interest. In earlier advertisements by the Medical Battery Company he is described as 'the eminent consulting Medical Electrician'. There were several companies in England and America which exploited the new interest in electrical appliances to produce what has been called 'the quack electric craze' which lasted from about 1880 to 1900. Few people had electricity in their homes and few really understood the meaning of the word. However, it had a certain magic quality and several firms flooded the market with highly advertised so-called 'electric' gadgets extolling their virtue as cures for a wide variety of complaints. Each firm used the name of a 'consultant'. There was C. B. Harness of the Electropathic Institute at 52 Oxford Street, London; Dr Carter Moffat of Imperial Mansions, also in Oxford Street; Dr Scott of the Pall Mall Electric Association of 21 Holborn Viaduct, London, 842 Broadway, New York, and Boulevard Haussman, Paris; Professor G. J. Baker of the Electropathic Association, 12 East Fourteenth Street, New York; and a number of others. Electric belts and corsets were the stock-in-trade ('a blessing to the languid and the weak') but electric toothbrushes, electric hairbrushes, electric flesh brushes, electric plasters and even electric cigarettes were all offered. The Harness firm advertised widely in such journals as *The Queen* and *The Illustrated London News* and also in theatre programmes. The Zander Institute of Soho Square which had advertised machines to encourage people to take exercise early in the 1880s appears to have been taken over by the Medical Battery Company in the 1890s.

Soap seems to have been as widely advertised in late Victorian times as washing powders are today. There was a cult of cleanliness among the middle classes which is hardly surprising since older people could still recall vividly the open sewers of London and the cholera epidemics of 1832 and 1848. Apart from this fact, soap was an essential commodity in each household. Nevertheless, there was a limit to the amount that could be used and in order to expand production one firm had to capture trade from another. Competition was therefore intense and consumers were subjected to a flood of advertising. In 1885 fifteen makers of soap and candles were already using the services of the United Telephone Company in London. These included A. & F. Pears of 38 Great Russell Street, WC, and Robert S. Hudson of 83 Worship Street, EC. Both these firms advertised extensively, though a Hudson advertise-

41 Day & Son bookmarker (c1890–1900) printed in black on thin card with an advertisement for the Electropathic and Zander Institute. Page-flap. Length 16.5cm.

42 Reverse side of Day & Son bookmarker above (41) printed in black on thin card with general advertising.

43 Reverse side of Day & Son bookmarker on page 31 (39) with an advertisement for 'Titan Patent Soap' made by the Liverpool Patent Soap Co Ltd.

41

42

43

ment has not yet been recorded on a bookmarker.

A number of household washing soaps appear on bookmarker advertisements, including Sunlight Soap (42), Titan Patent Soap (43) and Dr Lovelace's Soap (44). The greatest competition, however, was for the market in toilet soap. A. & F. Pears set the pace when Thomas J. Barratt became a partner in the firm in 1865. He raised the annual bill for advertising to over £100,000 in a relatively short period. New slogans were devised and in 1887 Pears bought a painting by Sir John Millais of a small boy blowing bubbles for 2,000 guineas and used it for their famous 'Bubbles' advertisement. It was Barratt who succeeded in persuading Henry Beecher Ward, one of the most famous of all American preachers, to provide him with a much quoted testimonial for soap which starts with the words 'If cleanliness is next to Godliness ... '

Pears registered designs for at least five coloured bookmarkers similar to the example (45) in which a hand forms the page-flap. Four other examples are illustrated in *The Saturday Book* for 1960, p 44. On one of these the hand points to the words 'Twenty highest awards 1851–1890', indicating that these markers were probably issued in the 1890s.

Not surprisingly, children feature in many soap advertisements. The child in the locket which hangs by a ribbon from a tablet of Wright's Coal Tar Soap (46) is a late and restrained example. Most earlier advertisements exploited popular prejudices. Pears even went to the length of painting a 'Pears' Soap is the Best' advertisement on a rock face in the Soudan which was used in an advertisement showing desert dwellers studying the strange tongue. Beneath it were the words:

'Even if our invasion of the Soudan has done nothing else it has at any rate left the Arab something to puzzle his fuzzy head over, for the legend
  PEARS' SOAP IS THE BEST
inscribed in huge white characters on the rock which marks the farthest point of our advance towards Berber will tax all the wits of the Dervishes of the Desert to translate.' Phil Robinson, *War Correspondent (in the Soudan) of the Daily Telegraph in London,* 1884.

44 *East Lancashire Soap Company bookmarker (c1916) printed on thin card in blue, brown, green and red with portraits of typical soldiers of Welsh, New Zealand and Indian regiments. Length 16.3cm.*
The reverse side gives a list of eighteen 'advantages and merits' of Dr Lovelace's Soap.

45 *Pears' Soap bookmarker (c1890–1900) with a page-flap in the form of a hand, printed on thin card in brown, green and red. Length 18.6cm.*
The reverse side states that 'the late Sir Erasmus Wilson F.R.S., President of the College of Surgeons wrote "Pears' Soap is a Balm for the Skin" '.

46 *Wright's Coal Tar Soap bookmarker (c1920) with page-flap, printed on thin card in blue, red and yellow with a grey border. Length 16.2cm.*
The reverse side is plain.

44

SONS OF
THE EMPIRE

WALES

NEW
ZEALAND

INDIA

With Compliments
Dr. LOVELACE'S
SOAP

45

PEARS'
SOAP

PEARS'
SOAP

The
Seal of Health
and
Purity

WRIGHT'S
COAL TAR
SOAP

WRIGHT'S
COAL TAR
SOAP
The Nursery Soap

46

G. H. Lee's Liverpool store is shown on a marker (47) as it was before World War I. Since then the ceilings on the top floor where the seamstresses worked have been raised. The four prominent windows were above ceiling height and were retained. The store has always been associated with the Oakeshot family.

The bookmarker showing a drum major of the Guards (48) is one of a series produced by the advertising firm of Pettys, London. The puzzle 'Find General Lockhart' gives it a topical flavour. (He is to be found within the busby when inverted, though hardly visible.) General Sir William Stephen Alexander Lockhart (1841–1900) served in India for most of his military career and rose to become a General in 1896. A year later he was sent to quell a rising of the tribes of Tirah and in 1898 became Commander-in-Chief, India. The bookmarker was issued when Lockhart's reputation was at its height.

By the time the bookmarker advertising 'Singer's New Sewing Machine' (49) was issued in 1899 the company had been selling machines for over thirty-five years. The first practical sewing-machine was made by the American inventor Isaac Merritt Singer in 1851. He founded a partnership with Edward Clark in 1852 which merged into a corporation, the Singer Manufacturing Company, New York, in 1863. The first electric machine appeared in 1889 but few homes had electricity at that time. The success of the firm owed much to the fact that it was a pioneer in the field of hire purchase. As early as 1856 it was possible to obtain a machine by making a deposit and a monthly payment.

The bookmarker (50) issued by Selick's of New York advertised their 'Florentine Cologne'. It was originally perfumed and still bears slight evidence of this. Eau-de-Cologne was used extensively in Victorian and Edwardian times. It was first made by two brothers in Italy, Johann Maria and Johann Baptiste Farina, from an extract of rosemary and bergamot with grape spirit. They settled in the German city of Cologne and called their perfume 'Eau-de-Cologne'. Selick's shop clearly attracted British tourists for the reverse side of the marker affirms: 'English money taken at full value'.

47 Bookmarker (c1910) printed in colour on stiff card with a view of G. H. Lee & Co's store in Liverpool. The traffic includes horse-drawn carriages and early motor cars. Length 15.3cm.

48 Bookmarker (c1896–8) printed in blue, red and yellow on thin card. Length 15.6cm.
The reverse side is printed in black with an advertisement for a boot and shoe shop—Frank Rose, 115 High Street, Stoke Newington, London. The publishers were Pettys Registered Adverts of which this is No 7925.

49 Singer Manufacturing Company bookmarker (1899) printed in green, pink and red on a thin grey-green card, with lettering in red. Length 16cm.
The reverse side carries advertising for a 'New Sewing Machine Insurance Plan' printed in brown.

50 Perfumed bookmarker (c1900) printed in brown, red and yellow on a blue-green ground with lettering in red. The stiff card carries an advertisement for a New York perfumer. Length 16.3cm.
The reverse side has the address of a steamship and ships' crew outfitter—Joseph Levy of 11th Avenue, New York.

LIVERPOOL

G.H. LEE & CO. L™
LIVERPOOL

· G. H. LEE & CO. LTD., BASNETT STREET, LIVERPOOL.

48

um-Major, Guards.

FIND GENERAL LOCKHART.

REGD. ADVERTS.   No. 7925

BOOK-MARK.

SINGER'S NEW SEWING MACHINE

PLAIN SEWING,
ART EMBROIDERY,
DARNING, &c, &c.
THE SAME MACHINE
· DOES ALL ·
WITH EQUAL EXCELLENCE.

Copy of Flower Subject
WORKED IN SILK ON
SINGER'S SEWING MACHINE

THE SINGER
MANUFACTURING Co
Branches Everywhere

Respecting our
NEW MACHINE INSURANCE PLAN

49

50

BOOKMARK

FLORENTINE
COLOGNE
C. H. SELICK
PERFUMER
NEW YORK

The Supex bookmarker (51) originally had a tear-off slip which could be posted to the firm by customers needing a price list of their products. Supex Limited was established in London in 1920 by Russian émigrés who took premises in Cork Street. They sold chocolates, tea and coffee (Russian blends) and 'celebrated thin, lace-like, deliciously crisp wafers — Crepes Dentelles "Gavotte", exquisitely suitable as friandises with dessert, tea, ice-cream, chocolate, wine etc'. Their products were advertised as produced 'according to old Russian processes' by the owners 'since they escaped from Russia'.

The design of the Bovril bookmark (54) of 1910 is ingenious and efforts were made to take out a patent. The girl's head on the sliding attachment can be moved up and down, making her eyes roll with pleasure.

Feltoe & Sons were sherry importers of Conduit Street, London, prior to 1874. Feltoe & Smith Ltd was a later partnership which issued the bookmarker (53), one of a number of firms making lime juice cordial, a popular drink in Victorian days. Stower's Lime Juice, for example, advertised in the *Illustrated London News* in 1891 and Montserrat Lime Juice in *The Graphic* in 1881. Competition was keen and it was not thought improper to denigrate one's rivals. The reverse side of the Feltoe marker tells us that the lime juice has no trace of the 'musty flavour which is so objectionable in most, if not all, other makes'. Feltoe's lime juice was not only 'supplied to the Houses of Parliament' but it received a testimonial from the Bishop of London (Dr Frederick Temple). Since Dr Temple was Bishop of London from 1885 to 1896 before he became Archbishop of Canterbury the bookmark can be dated to within this period. The marker quotes a letter from Fulham Palace in which the Bishop wrote: 'I have pleasure in letting Messrs Feltoe & Smith know that their Spécialité Lime Juice Cordial is highly appreciated by my family and friends.'

This was typical of Victorian advertising: every effort was made to persuade some eminent personage to express a complimentary opinion which could be quoted. · In this case there was probably little difficulty since a non-alcoholic beverage would be approved in most religious and temperance circles.

The bookmarker shaped like a Christmas cracker (52) is a particularly attractive example of its kind. It may well have been enclosed in a box of crackers in 1929 with the idea of getting an appropriate slogan for use in 1930.

51 Bookmarker by Supex Ltd (1920–5) printed on paper in brown, orange and gilt, to advertise chocolate. Length 12.7cm. The reverse side carries additional advertising and a 'Royal Appointment' coat of arms stating that Supex Ltd were 'Purveyors of Chocolate to H.M. King George V'.

52 Bookmarker (1929–30) printed in blue, brown, gold and red on thin card to advertise Tom Smith's Crackers. Length 17.3cm.
The reverse side gives Tom Smith's address as Wilson Street, London and carries the following offer:

'£5 offered for the best phrase describing Tom Smith's Crackers. Entries to reach us on or before March 31st, 1930. Enclose this bookmark with your suggestion.'

53 Bookmarker by Feltoe & Smith Ltd (c1890) printed in purple, red and yellow on thin card to advertise their lime juice cordial. Length 15.2cm.
The reverse side gives the address of the firm as Augustus Street, Regents Park, London NW, and includes advertising material and a testimonial.

54 Bookmarker by Bovril (1910) printed on thin card in black, brown, red and yellow, and fitted with a sliding panel which will move up and down. In the lower corner is printed 'No. 0292'. Length 17.5cm.
The reverse side bears Patent No 26245/10 but the patent application was abandoned and no patent was granted.

51

ESTABL IN LONDON 1920 — MADE IN ENGLAND

SUPEX CHOCOLATE — CHOCOLAT SUPEX

MADE IN ENGLAND · Шоколадъ Сюпэксъ · REG. TRADE MARK

SUPEX LIMITED
22 Cork Street,
LONDON, WI

SUPEX BOOK MARK

52

Tom Smith

53

BOOKMARK

FELTOE'S
SPÉCIALITÉ
LIME JUICE
CORDIAL
NO MUSTY FLAVOUR

P.T.O.

54

It must be BOVRIL

BOVRIL

I LOVE IT!

Bovril the BodyBuilder

Nº 0292

The transition from the penholder with nib and ink-bottle to the pen which carried its own reservoir of ink was a landmark in writing. The first reservoir pens unscrewed near the nib and were filled from a special glass filler with a rubber bulb which made it possible to suck the ink from the bottle and to expel it again into the pen. This was followed by the self-filling fountain pen as advertised on the Swan bookmarker (55) which was fitted with a rubber tube within the hollow shaft. This could be compressed by a small lever in the shaft when lifted. The nib was then immersed in the ink bottle and the lever depressed, the ink being drawn into the rubber reservoir. The reserve side of the marker has a close-up view of the 14-carat gold nib with which the pen was fitted, carrying the name of the makers—Mabie Todd. A white rectangle was left for the name of the retail stationer, in this case Lewis's Ltd of Liverpool.

The 'Parker Moderne' pen made by George S. Parker in Canada was advertised as an 'improved' type which was 'leverless'. The alternative to a lever was a plunger which could be operated by removing the end of the pen. Parker also offered two types of ink—*Permanent Quink* for records and *Washable Quink*. A strip cartoon used 'Brad', the precocious son of a family, to advertise the washable product. Since the marker states that 'prices do not apply in the Irish Free State' the date falls between 1922 and 1937 when a new constitution created the Republic of Eire.

The name 'St. James's Vellum' gives prestige value to the notepaper advertised on the bookmarker (57). The romantic view has St James's Palace as a background. The embattled brick clock-tower is part of the original building of the 1530s erected for Henry VIII. It then became the residence of the heir to the throne until the burning of Whitehall in 1868 caused the court to move to the palace. Charles II, James II, Mary II and the 'Old Pretender' were born at St James's Palace. In 1893 the Duke of York and Princess Victoria—Mary of Teck were married in the Chapel Royal and took up residence in the range of apartments known as York House. Ambassadors are still 'accredited to the Court of St James'.

55 Swan Pen bookmarker (1920s) printed in black on white card to advertise the 'Swan Safety Self-Filling Pen'. Length 16.5cm.

56 Parker Pen bookmarker (c1922–37) with strip cartoon printed in black on white card to advertise Quink inks. The retail stationer's name and address are printed in red. Length 17.6cm.
The reverse side carries an advertisement for Parker 'Premiere' and 'Moderne' pens, made in Canada.

57 Bookmarker (date unknown) printed in black on thin white card to advertise 'St. James's Vellum' notepaper. Length 17.8cm.
The reverse side is similar.

Pickfords carrier services started in the seventeenth century using packhorses which were often quicker than wagons owing to the poor state of the roads, especially in the north of England. In the south wheeled traffic was already well established and became very important for the transit of goods in the eighteenth century. The bookmarker (58) illustrates these two stages in the development of road transport and passes to the third—the early days of motor transport. There was, of course, an intermediate stage when the railways captured much of the goods traffic before the general use of the internal combustion engine.

The Great Western Railway, to take an example, came into being when a Bill that had passed through Parliament gained the Royal Assent on 31 August 1835. A hundred years later the company had expanded to 'serve Birmingham, Bristol, Exeter, Plymouth, Cornwall, Cardiff and South Wales', an area embracing some of the most attractive holiday districts in Britain. For years the railway had a virtual monopoly of the traffic to seaside resorts and tourist centres but in the 1920s the threat of road competition was already apparent. This was a significant period for the GWR. In 1921 Felix J. C. Pole became its dynamic general manager. In 1927 a new King class of locomotive was brought into service. The first of these, *King George*, broke all records and cut the time of the Cornish Riviera Express from London to Penzance to four hours. In the same year this locomotive was sent to America for the centenary celebrations of the Baltimore and Ohio Railroad.

The publicity which attended the new developments had been preceded by publicity to attract holiday-makers to the West Country resorts. The GWR became a publisher. *Holiday Haunts* extolled the attractions of the areas it served and so did the bookmarkers issued with it (59 and 60).

Scholarly illustrated books were also issued with descriptions of historic buildings—*Abbeys* (1925) by the Provost of Eton and *Castles* (1926) by Sir Charles Oman. The former, published in August 1925 had a first impression of 20,000 which sold quickly and there was a second impression of 20,000 in February 1926. In 1928 the GWR published *The Cornish Riviera* by S. P. B. Mais. After the resignation of Felix Pole in 1929 the holiday publicity tailed off and ceased with World War II.

Similar bookmarkers were issued by the French State Railways between the wars (61, 62 and 65). The dramatic example (61) illustrating an express train advertises *Les belles régions desserviés par les*

58 Pickfords bookmarker (c1905) printed in colour to advertise the firm's carrier service. Length 18.3cm. The reverse side gives the chief office as at 57 Gresham Street, London EC, and advertises summer holiday services; railway tickets, steamship tickets, summer and winter sports and cruises to be booked at the travel office, 156 Brompton Road, London SW.

59 Great Western Railway bookmarker (c1925-30) printed in dark brown on cream card with a view of St Michael's Mount, Cornwall. Length 18.2cm. The reverse side carries the coats of arms of London and Bristol and the following description:

'St. Michael's Mount, the great picturesque rock in Mount's Bay, Cornwall, crowned by an imposing castle and chapel, is one of the best known landmarks in all Europe. The tower, dating from the XIVth century, is part of a Benedictine Monastery, to which the adjacent chapel was attached. St. Michael's Mount, which rises to 250 feet, can be reached on foot at low tide.

STATION . . . PENZANCE.'

60 Great Western Railway bookmarker (c1925-30) printed in dark brown on cream card with a view of Valle Crucis Abbey, near Llangollen, Denbighshire. Length 18.2cm. The reverse side carries the coats of arms of London and Bristol and the following description:

'The Vale of Llangollen. One of the admired parts of North Wales is Llangollen, and its vale, which nestles in chains of "noble hills, the broader features of which are softened by gently rising knolls and swelling eminences", following the deviations of the silvery Dee. At romantic Llangollen, where the air is exhilarating one can climb Dinas Bran, court the tranquil beauties of Valle Crucis Abbey, fish for salmon in the Dee or tread the path George Borrow describes in his "Wild Wales".

STATION . . . LLANGOLLEN'

61 French bookmarker (1930s) printed on stiff card in black, orange and red with a picture 'after Helder' of a contemporary French 4-6-2 express with experimental streamlining. The marker advertises the railway network serving the tourist areas of Western France. Length 18.4cm. The reverse side describes the attractions of Normandy, Brittany and the South-west.

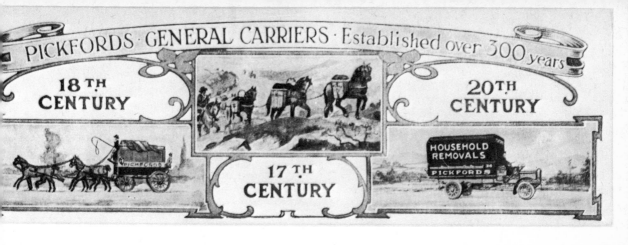

PICKFORDS · GENERAL CARRIERS · Established over 300 years

18TH CENTURY

17TH CENTURY

20TH CENTURY

HOUSEHOLD REMOVALS
PICKFORDS

Holiday Haunts Book Marker

Great Western Railway

Holiday Haunts Book Marker

Great Western Railway

61

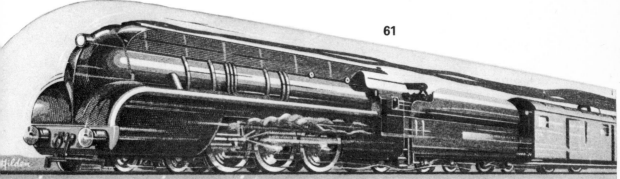

RÉSEAU DE L'ÉTAT · RÉSEAU DE LA MER ET DU TOURISME

Chemins de Fer de L'État which include Normandy, with its forests and ancient towns, Brittany with its menhirs, dolmens and churches, and the South-west with its historic chateaux and sunny beaches.

An earlier bookmarker in the Art Deco style (62/65) was issued by French Railways in the summer of 1929, advertising the circular tours available by *Services Automobiles*. A five-day tour from Dinard to Saint-Brieuc, Perros-Guirec, Morlaix, Morgat, Vannes and back to Dinard cost 450 francs.

The fashion bookmarker (63/64) from Drecoll of 130 Avenue des Champs-Élysées is probably pre-World War I, when Drecoll was one of the leading designers in Paris, vying with his contemporaries Doucet and Worth. The marker advertises '*robes, manteaux, fourrures, lingeries*', and was obviously issued to draw attention to his fashion shows, for on the reverse side it bears the words: '*présente chaque jour ses créations en son Hotel Particulier et a son Thé, rendez-vous des Parisiennes élégantes*'. Drecoll is described as '*nom magique, évocateur de suprême élégance et de raffinement*'. The marker also advertises his perfume: '*Tais-toi mon coeur*'.

62 French Railways bookmarker (1929) advertising circular tours in Brittany, printed on thin card in blue, green, pink and yellow by Prieur & Dubois, Puteaux. Length 17.6cm.

63 Gilt bookmarker by Drecoll of Paris (c1910) printed in black on stiff card, to publicise his fashion shows. Length 14cm.

64 Part of the reverse side of the Drecoll bookmarker (63).

65 Reverse side of French Railways bookmarker (62).

62

63

"LA ROBE„
par

DRECOLL

64

DRECOLL

130 AV. DES CHAMPS-ÉLYSÉES

PRÉSENTE CHAQUE JOUR

SES CRÉATIONS EN SON

∎ HOTEL PARTICULIER ∎

ET A SON

THÉ

∎ RENDEZ-VOUS DES ∎

PARISIENNES ÉLÉGANTES

65

CHEMINS DE FER DE L'ÉTAT
∘ ∘ ∘
Services Automobiles S.A.T.O.S.

Circuits touristiques
DE BRETAGNE

◎

"La Route de Bretagne"
en 5 jours
**Dinard, Saint-Brieuc,
Perros-Guirec,
Morlaix, Morgat,
Vannes,**
ou vice versa.
Prix : **450** *francs.*

◎

Service rapide sur le Circuit dit:
"La Route de Bretagne"
en 4 jours
**Dinard, Saint-Brieuc,
Perros-Guirec,
Morlaix, Vannes,
Dinard.**
Prix : **510** *francs.*

◎

Circuits de
Basse-Bretagne
des " *Cars Armoricains* "
excursion d'une journée.
4 itinéraires au départ
de Brest.
4 itinéraires au départ
de Morlaix.
Prix variant de **32** *à* **58** *fr.*
selon les circuits.

◎

*Renseignements gratuits et
détaillés dans les gares du
Réseau de l'Etat et bureaux
de tourisme des gares de
Paris-Saint-Lazare et
Paris-Montparnasse.*

Été 1929

PRIEUR & DUBOIS, PUTEAUX

INSURANCE COMPANY BOOKMARKERS

Between 1900 and the beginning of World War I many insurance companies used bookmarkers to encourage people to take up policies and some of them continued to use this form of advertising after the war.

The oldest insurance company in Britain is the Royal Exchange Assurance and they produced an interesting variety of markers. The earliest (67 and 66) show the period when horse-drawn carriages and horse trams were beginning to be replaced by motor transport. An interesting pre-World War I example (68) shows three Royal Exchange buildings, reflecting over four hundred years of history. The upper view depicts the first Royal Exchange initiated by Sir Richard Gresham (c1485–1549) who planned it as a *bourse*. His second son, Sir Thomas Gresham (c1519–79) founded the Exchange which was visited and named by Queen Elizabeth I in 1570. As a result many trading companies were formed and British trade expanded rapidly. In 1666 this building was destroyed in the Great Fire of London.

The second Royal Exchange was grander. It was designed by one of the City surveyors, Edward Jerman (d1668) and the foundation stone was laid by Charles II in 1667. It took two years to build. The stone was brought from Portland for the façade, and a striking feature was the tower in the Italian style. In 1779 the Royal Exchange Assurance Company made it their headquarters though it had been their head office since 1720. This second building was destroyed in 1838 by a fire which broke out in Lloyds coffee house.

The present Royal Exchange was designed by William Tite (1789–1893) and was opened by Queen Victoria in 1844. The eight Corinthian pillars which support the pediment over the entrance are 41ft high. When the building was completed the space in front was cleared for the erection of Sir Francis Chantrey's equestrian statue of the Duke of Wellington, who was present at the opening ceremony.

After World War I a column of Portland stone surmounted by a lion was erected between the Wellington statue and the main entrance to the Exchange, as a memorial to the London fighting men who lost their lives in the conflict. This may be seen in the later bookmark (69) as well as the entrance to the Bank Underground station.

66 Royal Exchange Assurance bookmarker (c1910) printed in colour on stiff card with a view of the Royal Exchange. Length 15.3cm.
The reverse side gives the name of the Governor as Sir Nevile Lubbock and a list of four London offices and twenty-two towns and cities with branches or district offices.

67 Royal Exchange Assurance Corporation bookmarker (c1900) printed in olive-green on cream card with a view of the Royal Exchange. Note the carriages and horse trams in the foreground. Length 15.6cm.

68 Royal Exchange Assurance bookmarker (c1912) printed in dark grey on stiff card with views of the three Royal Exchanges, completed in 1569, 1669 and 1844 respectively. Length 15.2cm.

69 Royal Exchange Assurance bookmarker (c1920–5) printed in black on grey card with a view of the Royal Exchange and the World War I memorial. Length 15.5cm.
The reverse side states that the 'Royal Exchange, London, had been the address of the Head Office of Royal Exchange Assurance 'for more than 200 years'.

67

ROYAL EXCHANGE ASSURANCE

Head Office,
ROYAL EXCHANGE
E.C.

FIRE · LIFE
MARINE
BURGLARY
Personal
Accident
Employers
Liability
Trustee &
Executor

FUNDS EXCEED £5,000,000.

ROYAL EXCHANGE ASSURANCE

A·D FIRST ROYAL EXCHANGE 1566 1720

FIRE LIFE

PRESENT ROYAL EXCHANGE 1844

MARINE ACCIDENT

SECOND ROYAL EXCHANGE 1669

TRUSTEE & EXECUTOR
ANNUITIES, BURGLARY, ACCIDENTS
EMPLOYERS LIABILITY
FIDELITY GUARANTEE
PLATE GLASS, MOTOR CAR

Head Office
ROYAL EXCHANGE E.C.

68

69

THE ROYAL EXCHANGE
LONDON
· · ·
Head Office of the
**ROYAL EXCHANGE
ASSURANCE**

INCORPORATED · A·D · 1720

The Scottish Widows' Fund was a Mutual Life Assurance Society founded in 1815. Early in the first decade of the nineteenth century it started to use bookmarker advertising on a large scale. The earliest type was produced when the funds stood at well over £10 million. This figure is printed on the bookmarker (70) with the engraving of a country scene. The reverse side of this marker carries a design which was used over a very long period. The lay-out which is *art nouveau* in style, embodies the Scottish thistle and has a medallion in the centre portraying a man clutching the mane of a winged horse (73). This is enclosed within a sickle, below which is a ribbon with the words: 'Take time by the forelock.'

This design was almost certainly by Walter Crane who later did a good deal of work for the Scottish Widows' Fund.

The second series of markers had colour reproductions of well-known oil paintings. Their rough sequence can be determined by the steady rise in the figures for funds in hand. The following examples have been recorded:

The Village Bridegroom, after Jean Baptiste Greuze.

St Paul's, after David Law, a Southampton landscape artist who moved to London in 1878 (71).

A Shop in Venice, after Borononi.

A Hostage, after E. Alvarez Dumont (72).

The Waefu' Heart, after Thomas Duncan RA, which was painted in 1841 and is now in the Victoria and Albert Museum.

Katie's Letter, after Haynes King, RBA, a London artist noted for domestic scenes who exhibited from 1855 to 93.

Dolly Varden, after W. P. Frith, CVO, RA, a picture, dated 1842, in the Victoria and Albert Museum. Dolly Varden is a character in Dickens's *Barnaby Rudge.*

June in the Austrian Tyrol, after John MacWhirter, RA, an Edinburgh artist who moved to London in 1880. This picture was exhibited in 1892 and was purchased by the Chantry Bequest for £800.

The Pool of London, after Vicat Cole, RA, a Portsmouth landscape artist.

70 Scottish Widows' Fund bookmarker (c1900 printed in black on thin card with an engraving of country scene. Length 17.9cm.

The reverse side carries a medallion designed b Walter Crane. Below it are the following words 'Persons intending to effect assurance should read th prospectus of this Mutual Society. Funds £10,750,000

71 Scottish Widows' Fund bookmarker (c1902) wit a coloured reproduction of 'St Paul's', after Davi Law. The art nouveau decoration on either side printed in blue. Length 17.5cm.

The reverse side gives a list of offices in London Glasgow, Liverpool, Manchester. Dublin, Belfas Bristol, Birmingham, Leeds and Newcastle, with th principal office at 9 St Andrew Square, Edinburgh.

72 Scottish Widows' Fund bookmarker (c1908) wit a coloured reproduction of 'A Hostage', after E Alvarez Dumont. Length 17.5cm.

The reverse side carries similar decoration to that o 71 above, but with the words :

'The largest British Mutual Life Office. Fund £18,500,000.'

50

ST. PAUL'S, *after* DAVID LAW

51

THE SCOTTISH WIDOWS' FUND

BOOK MARK

ALL PROFITS DIVIDED AMONG THE ASSURED

A HOSTAGE, *after* E. ALVAREZ DUMONT

Twelve bookmarkers depicting the months of the year were designed for the Scottish Widows' Fund by the famous designer, Walter Crane. They refer on the reverse sides to a forthcoming 'Bonus year' in 1913, so they were probably issued between 1910 and 1912 when the funds stood at well over £20 million.

Walter Crane (1845–1915) was born in Liverpool and was apprenticed to W. J. Lintot, a good engraver. Crane's first illustrated book, *The New Forest,* appeared in 1863 and he then produced a series of illustrated books for children including *The Baby's Opera* (1877). In the 1880s he formed a close association with William Morris and in 1884 became the first president of the Art Workers' Guild. In 1893 he was appointed Director of Design at Manchester Municipal School of Art, and five years later became Principal at the Royal College of Art, South Kensington.

The bookmarkers (74–76) must have been designed when he was over sixty years of age. They show what has been described as Crane's *horror vacui,* the urge to fill every part of his designs with some form of decoration, often symbolic. April (75), for example, shows the celandine, the first flower of spring, in each of the lower corners. Note that his work usually bears his monogram though it is not always easy to find. It normally consists of a letter 'W' within a larger 'C'. After 1900 Crane spent a great deal of his time writing and organising exhibitions.

This series of bookmarkers must have been reprinted for some record 'funds in hand' which have increased by £500,000 compared with those on the earlier issue. An offer was made by the Society to supply a set of these bookmarkers on request. Some of these sets may still exist in private hands but it should be possible for any collector to assemble a set over a period of time for these markers are not uncommon.

Those wishing to study the work of Walter Crane in detail are recommended to try to secure a copy of G. Konody's *The Art of Walter Crane* published in 1902.

73 Circular design by Walter Crane printed on the Scottish Widows' Fund bookmarkers from about 1900 until World War I. The winged horse representing Time is caught by the forelock by a symbolic Scottish Widows' Fund insurer. The sickle blade provides the 'C'– Crane's initial.

74 Scottish Widows' Fund bookmarker (c1910–12) printed in dark blue on thin card with a Walter Crane design depicting January. His monogram appears below the ice-sweeper's foot. Length 15.3cm.
The reverse side reports funds of £21 million and the 'Bonus Year' as 1913.

75 Scottish Widows' Fund bookmarker (c1910–12) printed in dark blue on thin card with a Walter Crane design depicting April. His monogram appears within a heart below the word 'April'. Length 15.3cm.

76 Scottish Widows' Fund bookmarker (c1913) printed in dark blue on thin card with a design by Walter Crane depicting November. His monogram appears on the left-hand side of the semicircular medallion. Length 15.3cm. The reverse side reports funds of £21½ million.

73

THIS is one of a Series
Designs by the famous
rtist, WALTER CRANE,
cially prepared for the

SCOTTISH WIDOWS'
FUND

FE ASSURANCE SOCIETY

he Complete Set may be
d free on application to

HEAD OFFICE:
NBURCH—9 ST. ANDREW SQUARE.

ONDON: 28 CORNHILL, E.C., AND
5 WATERLOO PLACE, S.W.

74

THIS is one of a Series
of Designs by the famous
Artist, WALTER CRANE,
specially prepared for the

SCOTTISH WIDOWS'
FUND

LIFE ASSURANCE SOCIETY

*The Complete Set may be
had free on application to*

HEAD OFFICE:
EDINBURGH—9 ST. ANDREW SQUARE.

LONDON: 28 CORNHILL, E.C., AND
5 WATERLOO PLACE, S.W.

75

Designed by Walter Crane for the

SCOTTISH
WIDOWS' FUND
(MUTUAL)
LIFE ASSURANCE SOCIETY

HEAD OFFICE:
EDINBURGH: 9 ST. ANDREW SQUARE.

LONDON OFFICES:
28 CORNHILL, E.C., & 5 WATERLOO PLACE, S.W.

DUBLIN . .	41 WESTMORELAND STREET
GLASGOW .	114 WEST GEORGE STREET
LIVERPOOL . .	48 CASTLE STREET
MANCHESTER . .	21 ALBERT SQUARE
BIRMINGHAM . .	12 BENNETT'S HILL
LEEDS . . .	21 PARK ROW
BELFAST . . .	2 HIGH STREET
BRISTOL . .	28 BALDWIN STREET
NEWCASTLE-ON-TYNE	12 GREY STREET

76

The Northern Assurance Company was founded in 1836. Towards the end of the nineteenth century it was known as 'The Northern and Aberdeen' and the accumulated funds had already topped £3 million. Most of the bookmarkers issued by this company are dated. A collection of eight of their markers covering a period of at least fifteen years reveals the following sequence:

c1898 A bookmarker with a yachting scene carries the name 'Northern of London and Aberdeen' (79). The accumulated funds stand at £4 million.

1903 Cream-coloured bookmarker printed in brown with a view of Aldeburgh, Suffolk. The reverse side carries a shield with a lion rampant against a stipple ground, the shield surmounted by a crown. Funds £6,523,000.

1906 Similar bookmarker with a view of the Thames and St Paul's Cathedral (77).

1907 Bookmarker with the same design as in 1906 but the name of the company has been changed from the 'Northern of London and Aberdeen' to the 'Northern'. Accumulated funds £7,089,000.

1908 Similar marker to 1907. Accumulated funds £7,198,000.

1909 Similar marker to 1908. Accumulated funds £7,436,000.

1911 Similar marker to 1909, but the reverse side shows a change in typography and the shield with lion rampant has a dark ground and is not surmounted by a crown. Accumulated funds £7,760,000.

1913 Similar marker to 1911. Accumulated funds £8,253,000.

An undated marker (80), probably of the 1930s, has a shield with the lion in red. The assets are given as £22 million.

77 Northern of London and Aberdeen bookmarker (1906) printed in brown on cream card with a view of the River Thames and St Paul's Cathedral. Length 17.8cm.

78 The reverse side of the above bookmarker (77).

79 Northern of London and Aberdeen bookmarker (c1898) printed in green on white card with a yachting scene. Length 18.1cm.

80 Northern Assurance Company bookmarker (1930s) printed in black, buff and red on white card. Length 15.7cm

77

Book Mark

78

Estd. 1836.

Persons about to **INSURE** *should choose the*

Northern

OF

LONDON & ABERDEEN

FIRE * LIFE
ACCIDENT
BURGLARY

Accumulated Funds
(1906)
£6,782,000.
Annual Income over
£1,700,000.

Moorgate St., London, E.C.

79

Book Mark

80

ESTD. 1836

THE

NORTHERN

ASSURANCE
CO. LTD.

Head Offices:

LONDON :
1 MOORGATE, E.C.2.

ABERDEEN :
1 UNION TERRACE.

ASSETS EXCEED
£22,000,000

*Every
class of risk
undertaken.*

What made the insurance companies so keen to use bookmarker advertising prior to World War I? It must first be remembered that the companies were very concerned about the future at this period. The possibility of a national scheme for the insurance of the working population was under discussion. It would be financed by employers, employed and the state. Despite the fact that many employers, especially those who had domestic servants, were strongly opposed to the Lloyd George insurance scheme, it was adopted in 1911. Against this background it is easy to see why the first decade of the century witnessed such a flood of insurance advertising. The companies wished to attract as much business as possible before the national scheme came in and bookmarkers were a very suitable publicity medium. Insurance was seldom 'a quick buy'. People had to think seriously about it since it involved commitments over a long period. Bookmarkers had an air of respectability. Reading was increasing with the spread of education. Bookmarkers would be seen again and again as people marked a page and later found it again.

It is interesting to note the emphasis on financial stability. Nearly all the bookmarkers give the date of establishment and state the company assets. There were, from time to time, take-overs, but the date of establishment in such cases is always given as that of the oldest company involved.

In addition to the insurance companies already mentioned, the following used bookmarker advertising:

The Eagle, Star & British Dominions, established in 1807 (84).

The Guardian Assurance Company, which started as the Guardian Royal Exchange in 1821 and took its present name in 1902 (87).

The Law, Union & Rock Insurance Company, established in 1806 (82).

The London & Lancashire Insurance Company, established in 1861 (85).

The North British & Mercantile Insurance Company, which started as the North British Insurance Company in 1809 and took its present name in 1862 (83).

The Prudential Assurance Company, established in 1848 (86).

The Rock Life Assurance Company, which was absorbed in 1906 into the Law, Union & Rock (82).

A valuable book in tracing the take-overs and amalgamations is the annual *Insurance Directory & Year Book* which gives a complete list of insurance

81 Rock Life Assurance Company bookmarker and paper knife (c1905) with page-flap, printed in dark brown on stiff card. Length 15.9cm.
The reverse side shows a lighthouse on a rock with the words: 'Stability', 'Security', 'Safety'. It gives the date of establishment of the company as 1806 and the address of the Chief Office as 15 New Bridge Street, London EC.
(Note how the exposed top has darkened with seventy years of exposure to dust.)

82 Law, Union & Rock Insurance Company bookmarker (c1910) printed in brown on thin card. Length 16.7cm.
The reverse side shows a figure of Justice in an archway flanked by Corinthian pillars, with the words: 'LAW · UNION · ROCK' on the pediment above. The foundation date is given as 1806, the total funds as £9½ million, and claims paid over as £25 million.

83 North British & Mercantile Insurance Company bookmarker (1903) printed in brown on stiff card. Length 15.6cm.
The reverse side is plain.

BOOK MARKER
AND

Paper Knife.

ROCK
LIFE
ASSURANCE COMPY
Established, 1806.

PAID IN CLAIMS,
Upwards of

£10,900,000.
FUNDS,
£2,935,155.

STATE DUTY POLICIES.

Low Premiums.

LEASEHOLD SINKING
FUND POLICIES.

Chief Office:
15, NEW BRIDGE ST,
LONDON, E.C

81

82

LAW UNION
& ROCK
INSURANCE COMPANY LIMITED

LIFE DEPARTMENT
Examples of Bonuses Added

Sum Assured £2000; duration 30 years;
increased by bonuses to £3323 : 16s.

Sum Assured £500; duration 20 years;
matured endowment; increased by
bonuses to £702 : 6s.

All With-Profit Policies participate equally,
and relatively to their duration and amount
would receive like additions.

THE AVERAGE **BONUS** DECLARED DURING
THE PAST TWENTY-FIVE YEARS HAS BEEN
AT THE EXCEPTIONALLY HIGH RATE OF

£1 : 16 : 5

PER ANNUM ON EACH £100 ASSURED.

LIFE.
*Capital, Funds, and Liabilities are by
Statute kept absolutely apart from
those of other Departments.*

FIRE.
ACCIDENT & SICKNESS.
FIDELITY GUARANTEE.
PLATE GLASS.
EMPLOYERS' LIABILITY.
DOMESTIC SERVANTS.
MOTOR CAR, &c.

---

*Before insuring elsewhere write for a
Prospectus to the Company at its*

HEAD OFFICES:

Old Serjeants' Inn,
Chancery Lane, London,

or to any of its Branch Offices or Agents,
and compare its **Premiums,
Profits, and Practice** with
those of any competing **Office.**

83

companies operating in the United Kingdom with the date when each company was established together with a list of amalgamations and of companies wound up.

Many small insurance companies have amalgamated over the years to create larger units. The Eagle, Star and British Dominions Insurance Company provides a good example. The Eagle Fire and Life Insurance Company was founded in 1807 after a meeting in Cole's Coffee-House, London. Between 1824 and 1856 it fused with twenty-one other insurance companies. In 1917 the Eagle amalgamated with the Star Life Company which had been founded in 1843 and took over the British Dominions General (established 1910) in the same year. From 1937 it became known as the Eagle Star Insurance Company and is now the Eagle Star Insurance Group.

The bookmarker of the Eagle, Star and British Dominions Company (84) is the most dramatic of all the insurance markers so far noted. It is the only one to include safety propaganda. The design shows a lighted cigarette which has fallen from an ashtray on to a table and the words: 'a little neglect may cause great mischief'. Below are two mock-Tudor suburban houses in flames, and a cutting from *The Evening News* with the headline:

Cigarette Did It
One-third of a Town Destroyed by Fire.

The history of the Eagle Company is told in A. F. Shepherd's *Links with the Past: A Brief Chronicle of the Public Service of a Noble Institution* (1917).

The London and Lancashire (85), Guardian (87) and Prudential (86) bookmarkers have a reassuring approach. The Prudential example can be dated from the printer's figures. In small type on the reverse side is the following: 'W.&S. – (6222) – 500. 8/30'. The 8/30 is the date of printing—August, 1930. Such figures are often to be found on printed ephemera and can be very useful for dating purposes.

84 Eagle, Star & British Dominions Fire Office bookmarker (1920s) printed in orange, red and yellow on paper with a scene showing a house fire caused by a lighted cigarette. Length 15.2cm.
The reverse side describes an 'All-In' policy for householders.

85 London & Lancashire Insurance Company calendar bookmarker (1929–30) printed in black and red on thin card. Length 15.3cm.
The reverse side advertises a householder's comprehensive policy.

86 Prudential Assurance Company bookmarker (1930) printed in red and black on thin card. Length 18cm.
The reverse side refers on the tear-off slip to the Prudential as 'the largest insurance institution in the British Empire'. The rest of the space is left plain with a heading 'Notes of books to read'.

87 Guardian Assurance Company bookmarker (c1930) printed on paper in blue, green and red with a medallion depicting a guardian angel. Other symbols are for Fire, Life, and the Sea. Length 14.2cm.
The reverse side advertises a plan for Life Assurance and states that 'the plan is equally suitable for ladies'.

85

THE
LONDON &
LANCASHIRE
INSURANCE Co
LTD

CALENDAR
1929   1930

84

a little neglect may cause great mischief

One Evening Dress
CIGARETTE DID IT

BRITISH DOMINIONS'
FIRE OFFICE

EAGLE   STAR &
BRITISH ✦ DOMINIONS
INSURANCE   COMPANY LTD.

TRACTIVE RATES FOR ALL CLASSES OF INSURANCE

HEAD OFFICE
BRITISH DOMINIONS HOUSE
ROYAL EXCHANGE AV. E.C.3

£20.000.000

Capital Subscribed £2,059,971
Capital Paid Up £1,024,578

Guardian
Assurance
Company Limited
Established 1821

Head Office
68, King William St
London, E.C.4.

The Company
transacts all
the principal
classes of
Insurance Business

Total Income £3,180,000
Total Funds £12,496,000

87

86

An Income of £200 a year
and a cash payment when you retire.

THAT is what a man aged 30 next birthday may secure at 65 by taking out an Endowment Assurance Guaranteed Bonus Policy with the Prudential.

The Annual Premium would be £35 8s. 4d. but allowing for Income Tax rebate at 2/- in the £, and assuming that the rate and conditions of rebate remain unchanged, the

EARLY OUTLAY
WOULD BE
£31 : 17 : 6
(LESS THAN 54 - A MONTH)

In the event of death at any time before 65

£1,000

with Guaranteed Bonus Additions of £30 a year (almost as much as the yearly outlay) would be available for his dependants.

IF YOU WOULD LIKE A GUARANTEED INCOME OF £200 A YEAR AT AGE 65 OR EARLIER, FILL IN & FORWARD THIS COUPON

To THE PRUDENTIAL ASSURANCE CO. Ltd.,
Holborn Bars, E.C.1.

Please send me particulars of an Endowment Assurance Policy with Guaranteed £3% Bonus which will enable me to secure an assured income of

£.............at age...... My age next birthday is .....

Name..................................
(Mr., Mrs., Miss)

Address..................................

....

....

BOOKMARKER MATERIALS

The practice of binding books with pages uncut which was common in late Victorian and Edwardian days made it necessary for the reader to slit the pages with a sharp instrument before the book could be read. Many bookmarkers were made so that they would also serve as paper cutters. A stiff card marker would sometimes serve the purpose but others were made of tortoise-shell, celluloid, wood, silver and other metals. The small tortoise-shell example (92) in which two tapering pieces of shell are joined to form a page-flap could be readily carried in pocket or handbag. Celluloid or 'artificial ivory', made by dissolving cellulose in acids and adding camphor, was particularly useful for making bookmarkers (88 and 89). The material was first made in the USA in 1870. It is tough, resilient and cheap to make but unfortunately is highly inflammable. Great ingenuity on the part of amateurs produced some unusual markers (90 and 93). The film-strip example was probably made as a souvenir. The most interesting of all souvenir markers are those made of sycamore wood. These souvenirs were made to be sold to visitors to resorts and tourist centres as early as the 1820s and the trade continued until about 1900. The peak of popularity was between 1860 and 1900. Several makers were involved in this trade but the most notable was the Scottish family of Smith at Mauchline, Ayrshire. The range of objects produced was enormous. Each carried a transfer-printed named scene. The view had first to be engraved on a metal plate. It was then printed on to paper and transferred to the wood by placing the print face-down on a shellacked surface. When dry the paper was sponged away leaving the print on the wood-ware. The scene on the bookmarker (91) is Gwrych Castle (near Abergele in north Denbighshire), a castellated mansion surrounded by grounds thickly wooded with pines and cypresses. When the transfer was made to this bookmarker the paper had to be folded over the edge so that the name 'Gwrych Castle' appears on the reverse side. It is one of nearly 500 scenes listed in one of Smith's travellers' albums entitled *Views for Sycamore Work*. No doubt others will be found on these wooden cutter-bookmarkers. A full account of these attractive sycamore souvenirs is given in E. H. and E. R. Pinto's book on *Tunbridge and Scottish Souvenir Woodware* (1970).

88 Imitation tortoise-shell bookmarker (c1900–10) made of celluloid printed in silver with bowl and text, the bowl overpainted in pink and green with flowers. Length 11.3cm.

89 Mudie's 'souvenir book mark & paper cutter' (c1905–10) made of celluloid with page-flap top. It is printed with an advertisement for their bookselling department. Length 8.5cm.
The reverse side advertises Mudie's Library (see p 74) and in small type is the name of the supplier: 'The Whitehead Manufacturing Co., 62 Fleet Street, London E.C. Made in U.S.A.'

90 Austrian bookmark (1930s) with dried flowers pressed between two strips of film stitched together with green thread. The word 'Seefeld' is painted on the film in white.

91 Sycamore bookmarker and paper cutter (c1880–90) transfer-printed with a view of Gwrych Castle. There is a page-flap. Length 16.5cm.

92 Bookmarker and paper cutter (1923) made of two tapering pieces of tortoise-shell clipped together with an electroplated metal mount of scallop shape. Patented 2 March 1923 by A. J. Smith of Variety Works, Frederick Street, Birmingham. Patent No on mount, 212101. Length 9.7cm.

93 Home-made copper bookmarker, impressed 1907, cut out in art nouveau style, in two parts joined by a cord. Length of longer part 9cm.

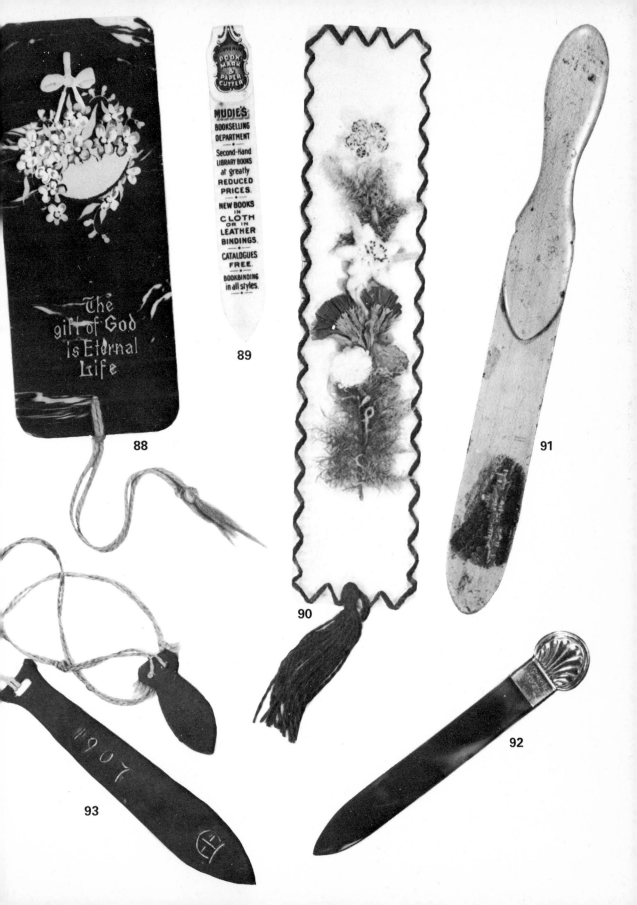

88

89

90

91

92

93

The gift of God is Eternal Life

#907

PUBLISHERS' BOOKMARKERS

Publishers in the 1890s found that bookmarkers provided an admirable advertising medium. They were able to list their forthcoming publications and their recent successes, knowing that each bookmarker would be handled many times. These bookmarkers give a fascinating survey of the popular authors of the day. They describe first editions of books now sought keenly by collectors and also of authors long since forgotten. A book collector should surely value a bookmarker describing the first issue of a book in his collection? Such markers should form an integral part of such a collection.

The books on the Methuen list of 6s novels (94) were all published prior to 1896, the probable date for the bookmarker. It includes several books which had made their authors famous—Marie Corelli's *The Sorrows of Satan* (1895), for example. Marie Corelli was then regarded as Britain's most popular novelist. Her real name was Mary Mackay. Stanley Weyman's *Under the Red Robe* (1894) was one of his famous romances of foreign adventure. It was later that he started to write novels with an English setting. The reverse side of the marker advertises a dozen new books including Gilbert Parker's *The Seats of the Mighty* (1896), a romance of the Anglo-French war of 1759 and his most famous novel.

The W. & R. Chambers bookmarker of 1899–1900 (96) offers books with prices ranging from 6s down to 6d. Chambers were publishers of books for boys and girls by several very prolific writers including L. T. Meade, the pen name of Elizabeth Thomasina Meade, who is said to have written over 250 stories for the young; George Manville Fenn, a schoolmaster who turned to writing and produced over 170 books; and Mary Louisa Molesworth, another prolific writer with over 100 books to her credit. The reverse side of the marker has a description of *Chambers's Journal* which had recently had contributions from Guy Boothby, Anthony Hope, Conan Doyle, E. W. Hornung and Sir Walter Besant.

The bookmarker by A. & C. Black (95) probably dates from about 1907–8, shortly after Sir John French became a general, and before he became Chief of the Imperial General Staff in 1912. The reverse side advertises two other reference books—the well-known *Writers' and Artists' Year Book* at 1s, and *The Englishwoman's Year Book and Directory* at 2s 6d.

94 Methuen bookmarker (1896) printed in black on mauve paper. Length 18.2cm.

95 A. & C. Black bookmarker (c1907–8) printed in orange and black on glossy paper. Length 18.3cm.

96 W. & R. Chambers bookmarker (1899–1900) printed in blue and black on thin card. Length 18.5cm.

95

Christian Bernard, Baron von Tauchnitz (1816–95), a Leipzig publisher, started to issue a *Library of British and American Authors* in the English language in 1841. These were cheap paperback reprints which he was licensed by the original publishers to produce for sale in Europe. It was stated on each copy that the book could 'not be introduced into Great Britain or her Colonies'. It was also proudly asserted that Tauchnitz editions could be purchased at 'all booksellers and all railway bookstalls on the Continent'. The main markets, however, were among English-speaking residents and travellers in France and Germany. If a traveller was discovered bringing a Tauchnitz edition into Britain, it was confiscated by the customs officials since this became an infringement of British copyright. However, the search of passengers' luggage was not always strict and many slipped through in suitcases and overcoat pockets, enough to ensure a large enough reservoir for the collector who seeks them today in second-hand bookshops.

The Tauchnitz bookmarker of 1907 (97 and 98) has an air of confident respectability with the American and British symbols in the coat of arms and the eagle.

When Baron von Tauchnitz died in 1895 over 3,000 titles had been published. By 1909 the number had risen to over 4,000, and in 1925 advertisements quoted a figure of 6,670 with 'more to follow'. Increasing travel to the Continent had no doubt increased demand. By this time British booksellers were expressing concern lest the Tauchnitz edition should damage the sale of the first British editions and efforts were made to delay the Tauchnitz reprints. However, the Tauchnitz firm was taken over by O. Brandstetter in 1934 and the threat was removed.

The speed of Tauchnitz publication is well reflected in the bookmarker. *Name of Garland* by W. Pett Ridge and *The Secret Agent* by Joseph Conrad were both published in England in 1907. By November of that year they became available in the Tauchnitz edition and the bookmarker quotes reviews from such publications as *The Saturday Review*, *The Spectator*, *The Times* and *The Pall Mall Gazette*.

97 Tauchnitz bookmarker for November 1907 printed in dark blue on thin card with notices of books to be published in their English paperback edition during the month. Length 16.4cm.

98 Reverse side of the same marker (97).

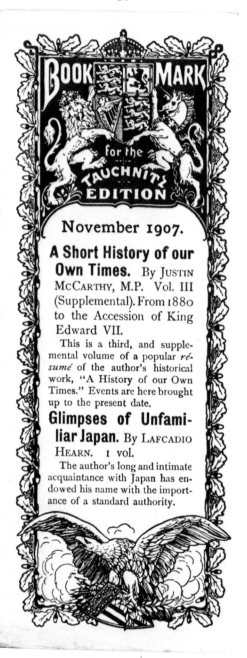

BOOK-MARK

for the

TAUCHNITZ EDITION

November 1907.

A Short History of our Own Times. By Justin McCarthy, M.P. Vol. III (Supplemental). From 1880 to the Accession of King Edward VII.

This is a third, and supplemental volume of a popular *résumé* of the author's historical work, "A History of our Own Times." Events are here brought up to the present date.

Glimpses of Unfamiliar Japan. By Lafcadio Hearn. 1 vol.

The author's long and intimate acquaintance with Japan has endowed his name with the importance of a standard authority.

BOOK-MARK

Name of Garland. By W. Pett Ridge. 1 vol.

"The story, with all its humour, has an undertone of real pathos."—*Athenæum.*

"Gay and irresistible humour at every turn."—*Pall Mall Gazette.*

"Mr. Pett Ridge has the secret of making his people natural and humorous."—*Tribune.*

The Secret Agent. By Joseph Conrad. 1 vol.

"A work rich in surprise and suspense, original in conception and treatment, lavishly endowed, in fine, with the singular qualities which have won for Mr. Conrad a unique position amongst the British novelists of to-day."—*Spectator.*

"The novel is more of a portrait gallery than a story, although it is a story, too, and a really exciting one. All the characters are made vivid, and their interaction is marvellously managed."—*Times.*

Arethusa. By F. Marion Crawford. 2 vols.

"Mr. Crawford describes for us a love-affair between Carlo Zeno, future grand-admiral of Venice... and Zoë, the adopted daughter of Michael Rhangabé. A breath from those riotous, cruel, gallant days comes into the story with these great names."—*Saturday Review.*

Laid up in Lavender. By Stanley J. Weyman. 1 vol.

Stories drawn from our own times, and replete with deep knowledge of human nature.

The price of each volume is 1 Mark 60 Pf., or 2 francs.

TAUCHNITZ EDITION.

Cheap Edition Bookmarkers

The foundation of the *Daily Mail* in 1896 was a landmark in British journalism. The paper sold at ½d and was launched as the result of the enterprise of Alfred Charles Harmsworth, later to become Viscount Northcliffe. During the first decade of the nineteenth century the 'Daily Mail Sixpenny Novels' were produced. They were extremely cheap even for Edwardian days. The Victorian 'yellow backs' which lasted well into this period had sold at 1s though these had paper boards for covers.

The folding bookmarker (c1910), which unfolds to form a single sheet, advertises the *Daily Mail* sixpenny novels and carries illustrations from the books of four popular authors of the day. Two of the illustrations are signed by H. M. Brock, a well-known book illustrator then in his thirties (99 and 100).

Among the authors then living whose books are advertised on the reverse side of the marker are Marjorie Bowen, Mary Elizabeth Braddon, Hall Caine, Arthur Conan Doyle, Beatrice Harraden, Maurice Hewlett, Robert Hichens, Anthony Hope, A. E. W. Mason, John Oxenham, Gilbert Parker, Max Pemberton, Arthur Quiller-Couch, W. Pett Ridge, H. A. Vachell and Stanley Weyman. This is a remarkable list, the more so since the average age to which these authors lived was nearly 76, an amazing longevity for men and women born in Victoria's reign.

The illustrations on this marker (99 and 100) were taken from the books of four living authors who had been particularly popular—Maurice Hewlett, whose first book, *The Forest Lovers* (1898), established him as a popular author; Robert Hichens, who wrote *The Garden of Allah* (1904), a novel which sold some 800,000 copies; Anthony Hope, the pen-name used by Sir Anthony H. Hawkins, famed for his cloak-and-dagger romances: *The Prisoner of Zenda* (1894) and *Rupert of Hentzau* (1898); and Stanley Weyman who was acclaimed for his first novel, *The House of the Wolf* (1890).

The Methuen sevenpennies advertised on the coloured bookmarker (101) were particularly good value for money. These were bound in red cloth boards and were of a size (17×11cm) which could readily be carried in the pocket.

99 Daily Mail folding bookmarker (c1910) printed in black on glossy paper with illustrations from their series of sixpenny novels. Length 20.3cm but the marker unfolds to form a sheet 12.7cm wide.
The reverse side of this sheet lists unabridged editions of forty-five copyright novels which are said to include 'only the best works of the foremost living novelists'.

100 Daily Mail folding bookmarker (99 above) showing the reverse side of the fold-over.

101 Methuen bookmarker (pre-1914) printed in blue, green, purple and red on thin card with an advertisement of their cloth-bound sevenpenny novels. Length 15cm.
The reverse side lists the first twenty-two volumes in the series.

USE THIS AS A
BOOKMARK

ILLUSTRATION FROM "THE HOUSE OF
THE WOLF," BY STANLEY WEYMAN.

ILLUSTRATION FROM "THE HEART OF
PRINCESS OSRA," BY ANTHONY HOPE.

METHUEN'S
SEVENPENNIES
Cloth Bound

LONE PINE
R B TOWNSHEND

BY STROKE
OF SWORD

THE POMP OF THE
LAVILETTES
SIR GILBERT PARKER

PROFIT & LOSS
JOHN OXENHAM

Methuen & Co Ltd.
36 Essex Street
London, W.C.

USE THIS AS A
BOOKMARK

ILLUSTRATION FROM "FELIX," BY
ROBERT HICHENS.

ILLUSTRATION FROM "LITTLE NOVELS
OF ITALY" BY MAURICE HEWLETT.

Publicity for Authors

Publishers' advertising on bookmarkers placed great emphasis on particular authors whose books were often sold throughout the English-speaking world. The Putnam marker with the view of New York (102) describes on the reverse side a single book by Cynthia Stockley—*The Claw* (1911), with an illustration of the actual book which has a Zulu shield and assegai on the cover and the sub-title 'A Story of South Africa'. There is also a review by James L. Ford of the *New York Herald* which refers to the 'innumerable touches of exquisite delicacy and naturalness' in this 'vivid and interesting story'.

Cynthia Stockley was born in South Africa, educated in England, and married in Rhodesia. She settled in England in 1898 and all her books were published after this date. She acted for a time with Frank Benson's Shakespeare Company.

The Story of Mankind (103) was published in 1921 and proved immensely popular, selling over 40,000 copies within six months. Hendrik Van Loon, the author, was born in Holland, went to the USA, and graduated at Cornell in 1905. He became a journalist and wrote a number of historical books including *The Fall of the Dutch Republic* (1913). He then turned to writing popular books, some of which he illustrated with his own rough sketches. *The Story of Mankind* (1921) was followed by *The Home of Mankind* (1933).

The South African bookmarker (104) was issued in October 1906. The printing of a monthly calendar, mail-boat arrival times and mail departure times ensured that it would be kept for reference and consulted frequently. The list of books on the reverse side reflects the tastes of the day. Successful new books included *Coniston* (1906) by Winston Churchill, regarded as the foremost American novelist of the period, and *Jungle* (1906), a story about the Chicago stockyards by Upton Sinclair.

Forthcoming books advertised in 1906 were Rider Haggard's *Benita* and Rudyard Kipling's *Puck of Pook's Hill*. Rider Haggard had special links with South Africa, which he visited in 1875, becoming in turn secretary to Sir Henry Bulwar, Governor of Natal, and then Registrar of the Transvaal High Court. He returned to England in 1880 and his first novel *Cetawayo and his White Neighbours* (1882) was greatly approved by the Cape politicians. Rudyard Kipling was already spending winters in South Africa disliking the climate of his Sussex home at Burwash. Other authors popular in South Africa in Edwardian days were Rosa N. Carey, H. G. Wells,

102 Bookmarker by Putnam of New York (c1911) with a view of 'The Skyline of Lower New York City from the Hudson River' printed in black and brown on thin card. Length 17.9cm.
The reverse side carries an advertisement of 'The Claw' by Cynthia Stockley.

103 Bookmarker by George Harrap & Co (c1921) printed in red and black on thin card to advertise Hendrik Van Loon's 'The Story of Mankind'. Length 16.8cm.

104 Calendar bookmarker and paper cutter (1906) printed in blue on stiff card in Durban, South Africa, for J. C. Juta & Co, bookseller of 430 West Street, Durban. Length 18.1cm.
The reverse side advertises some successful new books and also some forthcoming books.

105 Bookmarker by Dent & Sons (c1920) printed on buff paper in red and black to advertise their 'Everyman Library'. Length 16.5cm.

THE SKYLINE OF LOWER NEW YORK CITY, FROM THE HUDSON RIVER

Drawn by Edwin J. Meeker

103

104

105

Ue live under the Shadow of a gigantic Question Mark
WHO ARE WE?
WHERE DO WE COME FROM?
WHITHER ARE WE BOUND?
Read
THE STORY
OF MANKIND
By Hendrik Van Loon
HAS THRILLED THOUSANDS
— HARRAP —

DON'T
TURN THE
CORNERS DOWN.
Use JUTA'S
BOOK MARKER
AND
PAPER CUTTER.

OCTOBER.

S.	M.	T.	W.	Th.	F.	S.
	1	2	3	4	5	6
7	8	9	10	11	12	13
14	15	16	17	18	19	20
21	22	23	24	25	26	27
28	29	30	31	—	—	—

MAIL BOATS this month :
"WALMER" arrives Sunday, 7th.
"KINFAUNS" " " 14th.
"BRITON" " " 21st.
"KILDONAN" " " 28th.

ENGLISH MAIL
Closes SATURDAY, 12 midnight.
LATE FEE:
1d. until 4.45 p.m. SUNDAY.

J. C. JUTA & Co.,
430, WEST STREET,
DURBAN.

P.T.O.

A TALE WHICH
HOLDETH
CHILDREN FROM
PLAY AND ⅍
⅍ OLD MEN
FROM THE
⅍ CHIMNEY
CORNER
SIR PHILIP
SIDNEY
(See Overleaf)

Stanley Weyman and Mary Cholmondeley, wife of Lord Delamere, a pioneer settler in Kenya and a keen believer in white settlement. All these are included in the bookmarker advertisement.

The quotation from Sir Philip Sidney on the Dent marker (105) is the inscription used on the decorative frontispiece to volumes in the fiction section of their Everyman Library. The poetry and drama sections carried a portrait of Shelley and a quotation from his work. Bookmarkers were also used to publicise the *Everyman's Encyclopaedia* launched in 1913–14.

Methuen & Co probably issued the Joseph Conrad bookmarker (106) shortly after his death in 1924. The reverse side advertises among others *The Mirror of the Sea* (1906), *The Secret Agent* (1907), *Under Western Eyes* (1911), and *Chance* (1913).

When Iris Murdoch's novel, *An Unofficial Rose,* was published in 1962 Chatto & Windus took the opportunity of issuing a bookmarker (107) with a photograph and a brief biography of the author, listing also four of her other books: *Under the Net* (1954), *The Sandcastle* (1957), *The Bell* (1958) and *The Severed Head* (1961).

The Dickens bookmarker (108), issued with *The Sunday Companion* of 23 February 1924, is an interesting example of colour printing on cloth.

Many other bookmarkers have been issued with publicity for a particular book or a particular author. An edition of Tolstoy's *War and Peace* published in 1942 by Macmillan & Co Ltd with the Oxford University Press was sold with a bookmark which listed the principal characters, twenty-two in five family groups, together with a further twenty-one minor characters, a valuable service to any reader of this book.

In 1969 Adam and Charles Black issued a bookmarker to give advance publicity to the publication of Graham Webster's *The Roman Imperial Army*. In this case the bookmarker design was taken from the spine section of the dust-jacket to be used on the book.

106 Bookmarker by Methuen (c1925–30) printed in brown and green on thin card to draw attention to some of the novels written by Joseph Conrad. Length 15.4cm.
The reverse side lists six novels offered at 3s 6d each.

107 Bookmarker by Chatto & Windus (1962) printed in black and red, to mark the publication of Iris Murdoch's novel 'An Unofficial Rose'. Length 19.4cm.
The reverse side states that this book is a Book Society Choice and lists four of the author's other novels.

108 Dickens bookmarker (1924) with portraits of four of his characters printed in colour on thin cloth backed by card. Length 14cm.
The reverse side states: 'Presented with the Sunday Companion 23/2/24'.

106

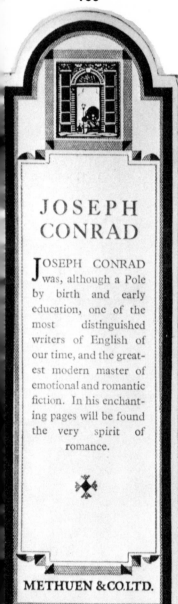

JOSEPH CONRAD

JOSEPH CONRAD was, although a Pole by birth and early education, one of the most distinguished writers of English of our time, and the greatest modern master of emotional and romantic fiction. In his enchanting pages will be found the very spirit of romance.

✦

METHUEN & CO.LTD.

107

Photo : Edmark

THE AUTHOR

IRIS MURDOCH comes of Anglo-Irish parentage and was born in Dublin. She was educated at Badminton School, Bristol and Somerville College, Oxford. After reading classical moderations and 'Greats' she entered the Treasury in 1942 as a temporary wartime civil servant. In 1944 she joined UNRRA and, shortly after the end of the war in Europe, went to Belgium, and then to Austria, where she worked finally in a Displaced Persons camp. 1947 to 1948 she spent in Cambridge, holding a studentship in Philosophy at Newnham College. In 1948 she returned to Oxford where she is now a Fellow and Tutor in Philosophy at St Anne's College. In 1956 she married Mr John Bayley.

CHATTO & WINDUS

108

WORLD WAR I BOOKMARKERS

The British government in 1914 soon realised that the war was likely to prove extremely costly if it continued for a long period. An hour's barrage on the Western Front cost as much as a whole campaign in previous centuries. Weapons of all kinds were becoming more intricate and expensive. In 1915 a committee was appointed to examine ideas on war loans for small investors and its recommendations were accepted by the government. The first War Savings Certificates were on sale on 21 February 1916 and in 1917 a National War Bonds Campaign was launched by the Prime Minister, the Rt Hon David Lloyd George. There was a dynamic publicity campaign which included the issue of bookmarkers (109 and 110). These reflected the need to curb public spending and to persuade individual citizens to save money to help the war effort. Various slogans appear on the reverse sides of these markers. 'Think before you Spend', 'Be a War Saver', and 'Will *you* devote your energies to increasing production and decreasing consumption to ease the burden of financing the war and bring prices down?'

It is ironic today to see a swastika on a British propaganda document, but the National War Savings Committee in 1917 could not know that within a few years the swastika would become the symbol of the German Nazi Party and the German national symbol in World War II.

After World War I the campaign to encourage saving flourished under the National Savings Committee (see p 86).

There were few advertising bookmarkers during the war owing to the shortage of paper and the need for economy. However, the example issued by Collins in 1917 is interesting because it reflects the wartime interests of the reading public (111).

Henry James, who became a British subject in 1915 and received the Order of Merit in 1916, died in February of that year leaving two long novels unfinished: *The Ivory Tower* and *The Sense of the Past*. These were published posthumously and head the Collins list of 1917. Then follows *Missing* by Mrs Humphrey Ward, described as 'a great novel of the war'. Francis Brett Young served with the Army Medical Corps during the war and his impression of the East African campaign, *Marching in Tanga*, is included.

109 National War Savings Committee bookmarker (1917) printed in black and green on stiff card. Length 17.1cm.
The triangular area with the swastika is a page-flap.

110 National War Savings Committee bookmarker (1917) printed in black and red on stiff card. Length 17.0cm.
The area covered by the War Savings Certificate book is a page-flap.

111 Bookmarker by W. Collins & Co (1917) printed in brown and green on thin card to advertise the books to be published shortly. Length 16.3cm.
The reverse side gives a list of the books.

COLLINS NEW BOOKS

AUTUMN 1917

LIST OF NEW PUBLICATIONS

NOVELS & GENERAL LITERATURE

W. COLLINS SONS & CO., LTD.

LONDON & GLASGOW

111

BOOKSELLERS' BOOKMARKERS

Many booksellers issue bookmarkers to advertise their stock, to indicate that they are willing to buy books, and sometimes to provide a map which will enable customers to find their premises which are often in side streets rather than main thoroughfares. Some take great trouble to make their markers attractive.

The Blackwell bookmarker (112) of the 1930s shows a print of Broad Street, Oxford, which was originally commissioned as a heading for notepaper. It was designed by E. H. New who was noted for his architectural drawings. Prior to World War I he had worked with C. R. Ashbee at the Essex House Press, Chipping Campden. In 1903 he illustrated the prospectus for one of their most ambitious projects—*The Prayer Book of King Edward VII*. The middle pages of the pamphlet had 'two of New's most peaceful woodcuts of Campden on quiet days'. (See C. Franklin. *The Private Presses*. 1969. p 74.) In the 1920s and 1930s New made a series of drawings of Oxford Colleges which were reproduced as prints, making a delightful record of architectural Oxford. He was also a book illustrator and made a series of drawings in the 1930s for an edition of Gilbert White's *Natural History of Selborne* published by Dent. He was also in demand as a designer of book-plates.

New's drawing indicated the 'site of the New Bodleian' which was designed by Sir Giles Gilbert Scott and built between 1937 and 1941, replacing some old houses. When the New Bodleian was completed Blackwell's found it necessary to change the view on their bookmarker (113). The work was entrusted to Wilfred Fairclough, an artist and engraver who was for some years Principal of the Kingston School of Art. By this time the bookshop had expanded and occupied Nos 48 to 51 Broad Street. Fairclough's design is still used on Blackwell's notepaper.

A recent bookmarker (114) issued in 1970 by a Manchester bookshop combines the functions of marker and blotter. The view of Mosley Street was drawn by Albin Trowski, an artist who was born in Poland and came to Britain during World War II to fight with the British Forces. He married a girl from Scotland and is now a successful commercial artist and teacher. From time to time he holds a one-man exhibition of his paintings.

112 Bookmarker by Blackwell's of Oxford (c1935–40), printed in black on cream-coloured paper with a view of part of Broad Street, Oxford, the Clarendon Building, and the site of the New Bodleian Library. The design is signed by E. H. New. Length 17cm.
The reverse side carries the statement that Blackwell's buy and sell books, and has a quotation from 'The Sunday Times': 'The famous bookshop where generations of undergraduates and graduates, poets and philistines alike, have browsed to their hearts' content undisturbed.'

113 Bookmarker by Blackwell's of Oxford (c1945), printed in black on cream-coloured card with a view of part of Broad Street, Oxford, the Clarendon Building, and the New Bodleian Library. The design is signed 'Fairclough'. Length 17.7cm.
The reverse side carries a verse by John Masefield.

114 Bookmark and blotter by Gibb's of Manchester (1970) printed in black on white card backed by pink blotting-paper. The marker carries a view of Mosley Street, Manchester, showing Gibbs's bookshop. The design is signed by Albin Trowski. Length 15.3cm.

12

13

LIBRARY BOOKMARKERS

Victorian times saw the spread of subscription libraries which became a common medium for distributing reading matter to the general public. These were sometimes linked to a book club, which enabled subscribers to buy books at reduced rates. Mudie's established their library in 1842 and combined it with a bookselling business. It lasted for nearly a century but finally sold its stock in 1937. Much of it was bought by Harrods who ran a library of their own. Mudie's issued a small celluloid bookmark and paper cutter as a souvenir (119) patented in 1905, and also paper bookmarkers (118). Subscription libraries flourished in late Victorian and Edwardian days. W. H. Smith were already operating a library at 186 Strand in the 1890s, *The Times* opened a book club and library at 93 New Bond Street in 1905, and the firms of Boots and Timothy Whites also established libraries. Boots and W. H. Smith combined their subscription tokens with bookmarkers (115 and 116) which could be attached to the spine of a book taken out by a subscriber either by using a long metal clip or by threading a cord through a small metal loop.

Many provincial department stores had libraries. Handleys of Southsea (121 and 122) is a good example. This firm started a library in 1919 which was taken over by The Times Library of Wigmore Street in the 1930s. Handleys' Library closed in 1955. The Times Library operated in a considerable number of department stores throughout World War II and into the 1950s. These served a useful purpose after the war when merchandise was in short supply, but were dropped by most stores as more goods became available on which a greater profit could be made than by lending books.

Between the wars there was a mushroom growth of 'twopenny libraries'. Many newsagents, tobacconists and confectioners kept a few shelves of books in their shops, mainly novels. A borrower paid a returnable deposit of 2s 6d on the first book, and could then borrow a book for 2d per week. The bookmarker issued by the Imperial Tobacco Company (120) was for use in tobacconists' shops, the reverse side being left blank for the local library advertisement.

The decline in most subscription libraries began in the 1950s when public libraries had established branches in many suburban districts.

115 Bookmarker and membership ticket for Boots Book-lovers Library (*1944*) printed in black on glossy card. Length 12.8cm.
The reverse side shows the subscriber's name.

116 Bookmarker and membership card for W. H. Smith's Subscription Library (*1958*) printed in blue on stiff glossy card. Length 6.8cm.
The reverse side shows the subscriber's name.

117 Timothy Whites Library bookmarker (*c1930*), printed in dark green on thin card. Length 17.7cm.
The reverse side states that their libraries 'contain all the latest novels'.

118 Mudie's Library bookmarker (*c1910*) printed in black on stiff paper with advertisements of new books on offer. Length 17cm.

119 Mudie's Library bookmarker and paper cutter (*c1905–10*) printed in black on celluloid. Length 8.6cm.

120 Imperial Tobacco Company bookmarker (*1930s*). Length 17.8cm.
The reverse side carries a rubber-stamped advertisement for 'The Croft Library. Thomas, 86 Stokes Croft, Bristol. Newspapers delivered to any address. Library books delivered.'

121 Library bookmarker issued by Handley's Department Store, Southsea (*1930s*) printed in black on stiff card. Length 13.9cm.

122 Handley's Circulating Library label (*1930s*) used in books to which their library bookmarker (*121*) was attached. Length 3.8cm.

115

118

116

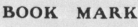

W.H. SMITH & SON'S *Library*
BRANCHES THROUGHOUT ENGLAND & WALES
W.H. SMITH & SON LTD. STRAND HOUSE, LONDON WC2.

117

TIMOTHY WHITES
LIBRARY.

~~S~~AVE
with
~~S~~AFETY

At

~~Ti~~mothy Whites
(1928). Ltd.

Renowned for

~~P~~URE DRUGS

and

Reliable

~~H~~ARDWARE.

~~Br~~anches Through~~out~~
~~th~~e South of Engla~~nd~~

BOOK MARK

MUDIE'S SELECT LIBRARY LIMITED

NIGHTCAPS

The Gentle Art of
Reading in Bed

Explained and Illustrated

By E. B. OSBORN

Excerpts from Old Favourites,
a Variety of Half-hour
Entertainments, a Selection
of Fables, e~~tc.~~

Crown 8v~~o~~

Pub~~lished~~

NE~~W~~

~~MUDIE~~'S

~~Depar~~tment,

~~..~~4

~~Str~~eet, W.C.1.

119

BOOK MARK & PAPER CUTTER

MUDIE'S
BOOKSELLING
DEPARTMENT

Second-Hand
LIBRARY BOOKS
at greatly
REDUCED
PRICES.

NEW BOOKS
IN
CLOTH
OR IN
LEATHER
BINDINGS.

CATALOGUES
FREE.

BOOKBINDING
in all styles.

120

OGDEN'S
St JULIEN
TOBACCO
COOL AND
FRAGRANT

ISSUED BY THE IMPERIAL TOBACCO CO. OF GREAT BRITAIN & IRELAND LT?

FASHIONS
FURNISHINGS
LADIES
& MENS
HAIRDRESSING
CAFE
LIBRARY
TRAVEL
BUREAU
SERVANTS
AGENCY

121

HANDLEY'S
Circulating Library
SOUTHSEA

122

Apart from the circulating libraries, a number of public and private libraries issued their own book-markers, sometimes with local advertising material. The bookmarker (123) issued by the Belfast Library and Society for Promoting Knowledge is a good example. Most of the space is covered with advertising but the terms of membership of the Society are fully set out and the statement is decorated with a reproduction of the library book-plate. This Society was founded in 1788 and took premises in the old eighteenth-century Linen Hall, over the main entrance. The Library, which had a collection of books on the linen industry, became known as the Linen Hall Library. When the Society was founded Belfast was making a determined effort to rival Dublin and Edinburgh as a centre for the arts and sciences, and the Society was a practical expression of this desire. The old Linen Hall no longer exists and the Society now has premises at 17 Donegal Square North. A fine engraving of the Linen Hall is reproduced in Dennis O'D. Hanna's *The Face of Ulster* (1952).

Local public libraries not only provide a service but also try to encourage people to use it. The puppet and the caption 'Seen any good shows lately?' on the library bookmarker (124) has a message to readers on the reverse side:

This world of ours is often drab and frequently reality is unpleasant. To turn, if only for a few moments, to the mere glitter and artificiality of the world of make-believe is good for every one of us—whether we be players or audience. For a moment, then, let us pull the strings, or see how others pull them. Whether your choice be a play, the film, ballet or comedy, you can read about it from conception to final production, and, if you wish to borrow the script to read by yourself or with friends YOU CAN GET IT AT THE LIBRARY.

Most library bookmarkers, however, give factual information and perhaps a little propaganda urging the public to care for the books. The fold-over bookmarker (125) from Weston-Super-Mare is an example. It carries this request: 'You are asked to take great care of the books and not to turn down the leaves but use this bookmark.'

Many libraries today have their own bookmarkers which are often used to advertise the Trustee Savings Bank.

123 Bookmarker of the Belfast Library and Society for Promoting Knowledge (1913) printed in black on thin white card with the terms of membership, and local advertising. Length 18.5cm.
The reverse side carries advertisements of 'leading business houses in Belfast'—The Carlton (Donegal Place); Cheyne's blouses (Grosvenor House, Wellington Place); Thos McLellan, Oculist (8 Castle Place); Weir & Sons, Silversmiths and Jewellers (33 Donegal Place); Ritchie's, Art Florists (51-5 High Street), and Milligan's Coal (18 Donegal Square). The bookmarker was supplied by The Wilson Advertising Co Ltd, Glasgow.

124 Kensington Public Libraries bookmarker (date unknown) printed in black and blue on paper. Length 16.9cm.
The reverse side gives a summary of the ways in which a library can help theatre-goers.

125 Weston-Super-Mare Public Library fold-over bookmarker (1939) printed in black on stiff green paper with hours of opening, details of facilities, and local advertising material. The marker was printed by Hearn's of Willesden, London, NW10. Length 19cm.

124

SEEN ANY
GOOD SHOWS
LATELY?

THEATRE AND CINEMA BOOKMARKERS

When London theatres returned to normal after World War II, the Society of West End Theatre Managers was anxious to revive interest in the stage, and started to issue lists of all the West End shows on paper bookmarkers. The example shown (126) gives the programmes for the week beginning 28 October 1946, and is the first edition. (Thereafter some 200,000 were printed each week to be distributed in theatre programmes.) This week Sid Field was at the Prince of Wales in *Piccadilly Hayride*, Gordon Harker at the Vaudeville in *Poltergeist* and Ronald Shiner at the Whitehall in *Worm's Eye View*. The markers continued for a relatively short period and were then replaced by the Theatre Guide as it is today.

In the 1960s The Times Bookshop, now no longer in existence, ran a Theatre Ticket Bureau which it advertised on bookmarkers given away with books sold in the shop (127).

Films have frequently been advertised on bookmarkers, sometimes by the circuit proprietors, sometimes by individual cinemas. The ABC circuit, for example, used a celluloid marker (129) to give advance publicity to the Warner Brothers film *Rhapsody in Blue*. The American composer and pianist George Gershwin wrote this famous rhapsody for piano and jazz orchestra as the result of a commission by Paul Whiteman in 1924. In 1931 he wrote a second rhapsody with the same title, which was less successful. After Gershwin's death in 1937 Warner Brothers decided to make a film about him, using the title of the rhapsody. It was produced by Jesse L. Lasky in 1945, with Robert Alda, Joan Leslie, Alexis Smith, Charles Coburn and Al Jolson.

Somerset Maugham's *The Razor's Edge*, one of his best known novels, was published in 1944, and two years later was made into a film by 20th Century Fox, under the direction of Darryl F. Zanuck. It had a notable cast, with Anne Baxter (who was awarded an Oscar for her performance), Frank Latimore, Herbert Marshall, John Payne, Tyrone Power, Gene Tierney, and Clifton Webb. The bookmarker (128) was distributed by W. H. Smith & Sons when the film was showing in Worthing, serving also to advertise some of Somerset Maugham's books.

126 Theatre Guide bookmarker (1946) printed in black and red on paper with a list of the theatre shows in the West End of London for the week beginning 28 October 1946. Length 18.9cm.
The reverse side continues the list.

127 The Times Bookshop bookmarker (1960s) advertising their theatre ticket bureau. Length 20.3cm.
The reverse side gives a list of the special Christmas shows including circuses, children's plays, pantomimes, ballet, and an ice show.

128 Cinema bookmarker (c1947) issued when Somerset Maugham's 'The Razor's Edge' was presented in Worthing, Sussex. Length 20.4cm.
The reverse side is plain.

129 Celluloid bookmarker with page-flap (c1946) printed in black and blue with material advertising the film 'Rhapsody in Blue'. Length 15.3cm.
The reverse side states: 'Coming to your local A.B.C. theatre shortly—"Rhapsody in Blue".'

EST-END THEATRE GUIDE

eek Oct. 28 to Nov. 2, 1946

DELPHI (Tem. 7611). Evgs. 7.
ts. Tu. & St., 2.30. Charles B.
chran's BIG BEN.

DWYCH (Tem. 6404). Evgs. 6.45.
. & St., 2.30. Robert Donat in
CH ADO ABOUT NOTHING.

MBASSADORS (Tem. 1171). Evgs.
. Mats. Tu. 2.30. St. 5.15 & 8.30.
EETEST AND LOWEST.

OLLO Evgs. (ex. St.) 6.45. Wd.
. St. 6 & 8.30. L. Banks, H. Bad-
ey in GRAND NATIONAL NIGHT.

OLLO (Ger. 2663) Nov. 4. 4 wks.
ile Littler presents RUTH DRAPER,
., Tu., Th., Fr., St. Mats. only 2.30.

MBRIDGE (Tem. 6056). DON PASC-
ALE with Stabile, Mn., Wd., Fr.,
LA BOHEME, Tu., Th., St. 7.0.

SINO Old Compton St., W.I. adj.
ace Th. (Ger. 6877). 6.45. Wd., St.,
. PICK-UP GIRL by Elsa Shelley.

LISEUM (Tem. 3161). Evgs. 6.45.
., Wd., Th., St., 2.30. Rbt. Nesbitt
d. THE NIGHT & THE LAUGHTR.

MEDY (Whi. 2578). 7.0 sharp. Tu.
St., 2.45. Claire Luce in VANITY
R, and Victoria Hopper.

VENT GARDEN 6.45. Mats. Sts.
, SADLER'S WELLS BALLET. Full
gramme Box Office (Tem. 7961).

ITERION (Whi. 3216). Evgs. 6.30.
St., 2.30. THE GUINEA-PIG, by
rren Chetham Strode.

CHESS (Tem. 8243). Evgs. 7.0.
St., 2.30. Flora Robson in
SSAGE FOR MARGARET.

KE OF YORK'S (Tem. 5122). 6.30.
St., 2.45. IS YOUR HONEY-
ON REALLY NECESSARY. 3rd Yr.

RTUNE (Tem. 2238). Opp. Drury
e Th. 6.45. Mats. Wd. & St., 2.30.
OLS RUSH IN. Cdy. by K. Horne.

OBE (Ger. 1592). Evgs. only. 6.30.
n Gielgud in CRIME AND
NISHMENT. Last Four Weeks.

YMARKET (Whi. 9832). 6.45. Wd.
St., 2.30. LADY WINDERMERE'S
N. By Oscar Wilde.

PODROME (Ger. 3272). 6.15. Wd.
t., 2.15. Tom Arnold presents Ivor
vello in PERCHANCE TO DREAM.

MAJESTY'S. Evgs. 7. Wed. 2.30.
5.30, 8.30. Arthur Askey in
LLOW THE GIRLS.

RIC (Ger. 3686). 7. Wd., St., 2.30.
Baddeley, W. Fitzgerald and
Williams in THE WINSLOW BOY.

P.T.O.

YOUR BOOKMARK

CHRISTMAS SHOWS

OUR THEATRE TICKET BUREAU can obtain the best seats for all the Christmas shows. A list of these appears overleaf; we are of course able to book seats for you at all the London theatres and concert halls.

Why not telephone WELbeck 3781 or write if you are unable to call at Wigmore Street (Ground floor).

THE ⚜ TIMES BOOKSHOP

THEATRE TICKET BUREAU

WIGMORE STREET LONDON W1

RHAPSODY in BLUE
The Jubilant Story of GEORGE GERSHWIN

CENTENARY BOOKMARKERS

Many organisations have issued bookmarkers to mark a centenary. The marker (130) gives a fascinating history of the development of public library services in the city of Oxford:

1854.	First library opened. Librarian: B. H. Blackwell.
1854–5.	26,991 readers.
1857.	First lending library opened.
1857–8.	7,371 books borrowed.
1896.	Central Library opened.
1896–7.	55,207 books issued.
1904.	69,891 books issued.
1932.	Bury Knowle Library opened.
1932–3.	630,149 books issued.
1940.	Temple Cowley Library opened.
1940–1.	1,119,915 books issued.
1953–4.	1,173,56? books issued. Librarian: J. P. Wells.

The Trades Union Congress bookmark (131) was distributed with a book: *The Martyrs of Tolpuddle*, published by the TUC General Council in 1934. The contributors included Walter M. Citrine, the General Secretary; Sidney and Beatrice Webb; the Hon Sir Stafford Cripps; Professor H. J. Laski; the Rt Hon J. R. Clynes; the Rt Hon Arthur Henderson, and G. D. H. Cole: a galaxy of Labour leaders and intellectuals.

The National Institute for the Blind, established in England as the result of work by Dr T. R. Armitage, a blind medical man, issued a bookmark (132) to mark the centenary of the invention of the Braille system of reading for the blind. Louis Braille, a Frenchman, was blinded while cutting leather in his father's shop, when a knife slipped and plunged into his eye. When he was fifteen, after deciphering texts in embossed letters and embossed messages in Morse code, he adapted what he had learned and produced a six-dot code in 1829 which was later widely adopted. In the year before this marker was produced over 600,000 publications in Braille were issued by the National Institute for the Blind.

The Florence Nightingale Hospital celebrated its centenary in 1950 (133). It 'is maintained to provide medical and surgical treatment for the women of the middle and professional classes of limited means, who cannot afford high fees and who do not wish to go into the General Ward of a hospital'. This was when Aneurin Bevan was Minister of Health!

130 Bookmarker (1954) printed in black on stiff cream paper to mark the centenary of the public library service in Oxford. Length 17.8cm.
The reverse side lists significant dates in the history of the service with the names of the officials in 1854 and 1954.

131 Bookmarker (1934) printed in blue on silvered white card for the Trades Union Congress, to mark the centenary celebrations of the Dorsetshire Labourers. Length 22.2cm.
It gives a provisional programme of events in which athletes from ten countries took part, and advertises the memorial volume 'The Martyrs of Tolpuddle'.

132 Bookmarker (1929) printed in brown on thin cream card to mark the centenary of the invention of the Braille system to enable the blind to read. Length 16.3cm.
The reverse side includes an appeal for donations.

133 Bookmarker (1950) printed in blue on thin grey card to mark the centenary of the Florence Nightingale Hospital. Length 17.7cm.
The reverse side states the objects of the hospital and includes an appeal for donations.

130

1854
1954

*With the
compliments
of the
Library Committee
on the occasion of the
Centenary
of the opening of the
first Library
1st June, 1854*

131

BOOKMARK

1834 — 1934

DORSETSHIRE LABOURERS' CENTENARY COMMEMORATIONS

✦

DORCHESTER
AUG. 30—SEPT. 2

132

BOOKMARKER

N·I·B

YOU ARE FOND of reading— will you enable the blind to enjoy similar pleasure?

This year is the Centenary of the invention of the Braille system by which the blind are enabled to read by the sense of touch. Will you mark this event by sending a dona-tion, and thus provide reading books for the blind?

The Blind *need* this Braille Book

133

Book Mark

Florence Nightingale Hospital
Founded 1850

First Lady Superintendent
Miss Florence Nightingale
appointed August 12th, 1853

"I ask and pray my friends who still remember me, not to let this sacred work languish and die for want of a little more money." —Florence Nightingale appealing in The Times for the Florence Nightingale Hospital in November, 1901

[see over

CHRISTMAS CARD BOOKMARKERS

Since the turn of the century relatively few book-markers have been produced to convey greetings, especially at Christmas and the New Year. Those that have been distributed almost invariably have secular themes; the days of the religious themes had ended. Some of the earliest greetings bookmarkers were printed by a firm called Mildmay which certainly existed before 1900 because W. H. Lever of 46 Aldersgate Street, London EC, advertised as a wholesale agent for Mildmay's in 1890 (see G. Buday. *The History of the Christmas Card*. 1964. p 274). The marker with a view of Brougham Castle (134) has a tear-off Christmas greetings slip and the reverse side has a calendar for 1909. (Brougham Castle is in the north of Westmorland, two miles south-east of Penrith.) A similar calendar bookmark for 1927 bearing New Year greetings with the mark 'Mildmay No. 1477' has been noted suggesting that the Mildmay series extended over a period of years.

In the 1930s there was a craze for leatherwork. Classes were held to teach students to make book-markers, purses, handbags and other small articles. Leather was cut from a skin and sewn together with thin leather laces. So popular was this craft that paper imitations appeared. The bookmarker (136) dated 1942 uses a leatherwork pattern on stiff brown card. Very many bookmarkers of this period were made of similar card to simulate leather.

The 1950s saw a great increase in the output of greetings bookmarks. Some were embossed and carried gilt initials. Others folded like a Christmas card and could have the name and address of the sender printed inside (135); others carried a calendar (137). Occasionally these markers carry the name of the maker. Manufacturers noted include:

The Medici Society of London and New York, which issued a series of pictorial bookmarks in the 1920s.

Newton Mill Ltd, Manufacturing Stationers of 9 Argyle Street, London, who produced a series of 'Waldorf' greetings cards.

Raphael Tuck, a firm which has been in business since the 1870s. It established a New York branch in 1885, and produced Christmas cards for Queen Victoria in the 1890s. Their trade mark is an artist's easel.

Valentine & Sons Ltd, of Dundee and Morris House, Berkeley Square, London, who produced a 'De Luxe' series of bookmarkers.

134 *Mildmay calendar bookmarker (1909) printed in green and brown on cream card with a view of Brougham Castle. Length (with tear-off greetings section) 19.1cm. The reverse side carries a calendar for 1909.*

135 *Christmas card folding bookmarker (1956) printed in black, blue and gilt on white card. Inside is a privately printed Christmas greeting from Duffield, Derbyshire, signed and dated by the sender. Length 17cm.*

136 *Greetings card (1942) printed in brown, red and yellow on stiff brown card with a design imitating a leather craftwork bookmarker. Length 20.4cm. The reverse side has a handwritten greeting dated 1942.*

137 *Raphael Tuck calendar bookmarker (1952) printed in dark green on light green card. A colour print of a cottage garden has been pasted on to form an oval medallion. Length 19.1cm.*

134

135

Each page records Old Times, Old Friends and in Remembrance a Greeting sends

136

I count myself in nothing else so happy As in a soul remembering my good friends.
Shakespeare.

137

Book Mark

CALENDAR

WORLD WAR II BOOKMARKERS

Relatively few bookmarkers were printed between 1939 and 1945 owing to paper restrictions, but some official ones were issued with the object of strengthening the determination of the British people to win the war against Nazi Germany. At least six different markers were printed in July 1941, each with the same statement on the reverse side (see caption 138).

The Spitfires and Hurricanes (138) had already proved themselves in the Battle of Britain. The Spitfire Mark I was a single-seater fighter with a Rolls Royce Merlin engine. It was armed with eight Browning machine-guns, four in each wing, and the maximum speed was 366 mph. The Hawker Hurricane Mark I was similarly equipped and had a maximum speed of 335 mph. During the Middle East campaign the Hurricane was used as a fighter-bomber. It had the advantage that it could protect itself, aim accurately, and could be diverted very quickly to protect heavy bombers.

The battleship HMS *Nelson* (140) was laid down in 1922. During the war she operated off the coast of Norway, attacking enemy shipping in September 1940 and covering the attack on the Lofoten Islands in March 1941. Later she became an escort vessel for convoys to West Africa and the Mediterranean.

During the Normandy landings in June 1944 HMS *Nelson* was involved in twenty bombardments, and after receiving some damage went to the USA to refit before starting a period of duty with the East Indies Fleet off Malaya. She was present at Singapore when the Japanese forces in south-east Asia surrendered. After the war HMS *Nelson* became a training battleship and in 1948 was broken up.

Other markers in this series show 'Britain's Mechanised Might', a photograph of tanks in action; 'Spectacular Take-off', a Sunderland flying-boat or 'Flying Battleship'; 'The Bull-Dog Breed', showing men of a famous British Regiment with the 'deadly Thompson sub-machine gun'; and a night study of British anti-aircraft guns putting up a barrage against Nazi raiders. There may well have been others. If so, they will no doubt be traced by collectors.

The YWCA bookmarker (139) represents a receipt for 3d given to the Lord Mayor of London's War-time Appeal which was registered under the War Charities Act 1940. The President was Mrs Churchill, CBE.

138 Official World War II bookmarker (1941), printed in black on thin card by Fosh & Cross Ltd, showing Spitfire and Hurricane fighter planes. Length 17.1cm. The reverse side has the following simple statement: 'BRITAIN AND HER ALLIES ARE RESOLVED ON THIS ** *that come what may the menace of a world ruled by force alone shall be lifted from the hearts of men by the strength of those who stand for* FREEDOM.'

139 Bookmarker (c1940) printed on paper in blue and black, appealing for funds for the Young Women's Christian Association War-Time Fund to help provide canteen clubs, mobile clubs, land army hostels and industrial hostels. Length 15.7cm. The reverse side has the serial number 17186.

140 Official World War II bookmarker (1941) printed in black on thin card by Fosh & Cross Ltd, showing 'HMS Nelson' at sea. Length 17.1cm. Reverse side as on (138) above.

IMMORTAL FAME has been gained by the gallant and skilful fighter-pilots of Britain's Royal Air Force. Above the lanes and fields of their homeland, the superb " Spitfires " (above) and " Hurricanes " (below), with their high speed combined with manoeuvrability, have shot down nearly three thousand Nazi machines, over 7,000 Nazi airmen, for a loss of only 800 British machines and 400 of their brave pilots.

138

ONE HUT COSTS £3,500

HOW MUCH WILL YOU GIVE? Y.W.C.A.

Thank You for Your Gift

TO THE 3D

Y.W.C.A.

" H.M.S. NELSON," a great British battleship which carries nine 16-inch guns. These huge weapons of destruction hurl a devastating broadside of some nine tons of high-explosive across a distance of fifteen to twenty miles. Everything on a battleship is designed in relation to the big guns—for feeding, protecting, transporting, aiming and firing them.

140

NATIONAL SAVINGS BOOKMARKERS

Between the two World Wars bookmarkers were used extensively to encourage thrift. When World War I was over, the National Savings Movement, which grew out of the War Savings Campaign (see p 70), began to lose ground. In 1923 there were only 18,400 savings groups in existence compared with 41,000 in 1919. After this the position improved, for, despite the General Strike of 1926 and the world depression of trade and employment that followed the American financial crisis of 1929, the Movement stuck doggedly to its job of promoting thrift. By 1939 small savings had reached a record level. The amount standing to the credit of small investors in National Savings was £1,500 million compared with £870 million in 1919. Throughout the period from 1923 to 1939 bookmarkers provided a useful medium of publicity as voluntary groups and committees were formed throughout the country. There was nothing brash about the publicity. There was always the suggestion of something to look forward to in the future, sun in the countryside (143), holidays at home (142) or abroad (144), or a contented old age (141). 'The journey of a thousand miles begins with one step' states one of the markers, quoting Lao-tze.

All the National Savings bookmarkers carry a number. There were two main series. The first five, of which the contented cat (141) is a good example, all bear numbers between 432 and 487. These were 432, 433 and 434 published in February 1923; 470 in November 1928, and 487 in October 1929. The second series all start with the letters NS. These are as follows: NS1, October 1930; NS 5, November 1930; NS 20, January 1932; NS 33, October 1933 (142); NS 41, August 1934 (143); NS 57 and NS 57W, July 1936; NS 75, June 1938 (144); and NS 76, June 1939 (145). After this date only one more bookmarker was published: SL 486 in March 1969.

141 *National Savings bookmarker No 487 (1929) printed in browns and red on thin card with a cat as a symbol of contentment. Length 17cm.*
The reverse side urges investment in National Savings.

142 *National Savings bookmarker No 33 (1933) printed in blue, green and orange on thin card with a view of a couple on a cliff-top. The marker was issued by the Liverpool Committee for National Savings. Length 17cm.*
The reverse side urges saving in National Savings Certificates, the Post Office Savings Bank and Trustee Savings Banks.

143 *National Savings bookmarker No 41 (1934) printed in blue, green and red on thin card with a view of trees. The view is initialled 'J.F.R.' and below is a verse from W. H. Davies. Length 17cm.*
Reverse side as on (141) above.

144 *National Savings bookmarker No 75 (1938) printed in blue, brown and green on thin card with a view of a lake. Length 17.2cm.*
Reverse side similar to (141) above.

145 *National Savings bookmarker No 76 (1939) printed in blue, green, orange, red and yellow, with fruits and flowers symbolic of the four seasons. Length 17.3cm.*
Reverse side similar to (141) above.

143

141

CONTENT

BETTER
PROSPECTS
IN YOUTH AND
GREATER COMFORT
IN OLD AGE
BUY
Savings
CERTIFICATES

144

NATIONAL
SAVINGS
will give you
a
WIDER
HORIZON

HOLIDAYS   CLOTHES
FOR SICKNESS   FOR NEST EGGS
JOIN A SAVINGS ASSOCIATION

PARTICULARS
GLADLY SUPPLIED BY
LIVERPOOL COMMITTEE
FOR NATIONAL SAVINGS
20, SIR THOMAS
STREET
LIVERPOOL, 1

142

NATIONAL   SAVINGS

ALL
THE
YEAR
ROUND

145

HEALTH AND SAFETY BOOKMARKERS

The well-known slogan 'Coughs and Sneezes Spread Diseases' originated on a Ministry of Health poster in 1945. It was important at this time to maintain a high level of production in factories and workshops by reducing the incidence of minor illnesses and the spread of any influenza epidemic. The bookmarker (146) gives no clue as to its origin but almost certainly formed part of the Ministry's health propaganda.

Bookmarkers have been used by the Royal Society for the Prevention of Accidents to disseminate road safety propaganda for more than twenty years, urging pedestrians to use crossings, and cyclists and motorists to honour the Highway Code.

One bookmarker (147) shows a pedestrian crossing illuminated by amber globes on black and white posts. These crossings were first introduced by Leslie Hore-Belisha in 1934 when he moved from his post as financial secretary to the Treasury to be the Minister of Transport soon after the Road Traffic Act had received its Third Reading. He quickly took action and extended the use of pedestrian crossings with their flashing lights which came to be known as 'Belisha Beacons'.

Perhaps the most interesting of these bookmarkers is the one which uses characters from a Walt Disney cartoon showing Donald Duck with the dog Pluto on a lead (149). The first talking picture by Walt Disney was of Mickey Mouse in *Steamboat Willie*, shown in 1929. It was an immediate success and Disney received a special citation in 1932 as the creator of Mickey Mouse, who continued to appear until 1941. A 'comic' paper, *The Mickey Mouse Weekly*, was published early in 1936, the first in full-colour photogravure. There were twelve pages and it sold for 2d. Other Disney characters followed including the well-known Donald Duck and Pluto. The marker using these characters could not fail to draw attention to itself, especially the attention of children.

All these bookmarkers were left plain on the reverse side so that local road-safety committees could use it for information and propaganda.

146 Health propaganda bookmarker (c1945) printed in blue, red and yellow with the famous 'coughs and sneezes spread diseases' slogan. Length 19cm.
The reverse side gives advice about 'The War against Colds and "Flu" '.

147 Royal Society for the Prevention of Accidents bookmarker (1950s) printed on thin card in black, blue and orange, with a Belisha pedestrian crossing and the advice: 'Drivers observe, pedestrians use the proper crossing.' Length 16.8cm.
The reverse side is plain.

148 Royal Society for the Prevention of Accidents bookmarker (1950s) printed on thin card in black, blue and red, stressing the need to observe the Highway Code. Length 14.7cm.
The reverse side is plain.

149 Royal Society for the Prevention of Accidents bookmarker (1950s) printed on thin card in black and green with a Walt Disney cartoon showing Donald Duck holding Pluto on a lead. Length 14.2cm.
The reverse side has a rubber-stamp mark: 'Issued by Borough of Weston-Super-Mare Road Safety Committee.'
(Reproduced by courtesy of Walt Disney Productions Ltd.)

148

146

147

149

TOURIST SOUVENIR BOOKMARKERS

Museum bookmarkers are not common. The example carrying the imprint of the Metropolitan Museum of Art, New York (150) shows *Flowers and Berries*, a Chinese wood-block print, after a painting by the Empress Dowager Tz'u Hsi (1834–1908).

The souvenir bookmarker with the views of Prinknash Abbey (151) is one of a series issued by Friths. Prinknash Abbey is about three miles southeast of Gloucester, on a slope of the Cotswold Hills. In 1520 a mansion was built at Prinknash which became the country seat of the Abbots of Gloucester. At the Dissolution it passed into private hands but in the 1920s the mansion was given by the Earl of Rothes to some Benedictine monks who had previously lived on Caldy Island, near Tenby. In 1938 Prinknash became an abbey and the monks started to build an abbey church beside the old mansion, which had been reconstructed to serve its new function. Another bookmarker of this type shows views of West Hartlepool.

The Inverewe bookmarker (152) has an interesting design intended to draw attention to the Inverewe Gardens, Wester Ross. The site on which they have been laid out is on the coast at the head of Loch Ewe, about seven miles from Gairloch. It was bought by Osgood Mackenzie in 1862 and consisted of red sandstone rock and peat, almost devoid of vegetation except for some stunted heather and crowberry. Mackenzie had inherited a love of trees and flowers from his father and grandfather who were Lairds of Gairloch. He saw the possibilities of the site, for the warm coastal waters give a remarkably mild climate to the area, despite the high latitude (57°45′N). However, many tons of good soil had to be brought to the gardens in creels, the osier baskets normally used for carrying fish. A deer and rabbit fence was erected to enclose the area, and a belt of Corsican pine and Scots fir was planted to protect the gardens from strong Atlantic gales. Then hedges of rhododendron were established, and finally many plants were brought from Australia, South America and New Zealand, including many rare species.

Osgood Mackenzie died in 1922 but his daughter, Mrs Mairi T. Sawyer continued the work until 1952, a year before her death, when she presented Inverewe Gardens to the National Trust for Scotland with an endowment for its upkeep. The gardens are at their best in May, June and July but at no time of year are they without flowers.

150 Museum bookmarker (date unknown) printed in black from a Chinese wood-block, for the Metropolitan Museum of Art, New York. Length 18.1cm.
The reverse side gives the title of the original painting from which it was taken, with the name of the artist.

151 Souvenir bookmarker by Friths (c1945–50) consisting of a series of photographic reproductions of Prinknash Abbey, Gloucestershire, enclosed between two strips of film to which is attached a yellow tassel. Length 16.4cm.
The reverse side is similar but shows five different views of Prinknash Abbey, and has the words: 'Bookmark by Friths'.

152 Bookmark by the National Trust for Scotland (1968) printed on thin card in black, grey, orange and purple, to draw attention to Inverewe Gardens, Wester Ross. Length 17.7cm.
The reverse side gives a brief description of the gardens.

150

151

152

MODERN BOOKMARKERS

The giving of book tokens has increased enormously in recent years and the annual turnover now tops £2 million. Considerable numbers of book tokens are given to children—32 per cent to children under twelve, and another 12 per cent to teenagers between thirteen and seventeen. The tokens themselves are extremely attractive. Those for the younger children have coloured pictures of Rupert Bear, Dougal, and the Toytown police station, and these are illustrated on the bookmarker (153) issued to publicise the service.

Penguin Books issue monthly bookmarkers (155) which carry a design on one side and a selection of new books on the other. They are stocked by most booksellers.

On 11 December 1973 Scottish Opera held its 600th performance and marked the occasion by presenting a bookmarker (154) to each member of the audience at a revival of their *La Traviata* production in Edinburgh. The marker was designed by David Gray who lives and works in Glasgow. Scottish Opera was founded in 1962 by Alexander Gibson, and since then has presented over forty different operas. The climax of the company's first ten years was a complete cycle of Wagner's *Ring* given in Glasgow in 1971. In August 1973 the Scottish Opera paid its first visit to London, taking a repertoire of *Tristan und Isolde* and *Pelleas and Melisande* to Sadler's Wells Theatre.

The small bookmarker (156), which carries the word 'Bookmark' in decorative lettering, comes to members of The Folio Society as a tear-off strip on a reply-paid postcard intended for those who wish to introduce a friend to the Society. An enquiry about the designer produced this reply from Mr John Letts:

'You will be amused to hear that the designer responsible for this bookmark was in fact myself, and that I put it together in half an hour over one lunch hour, when our designer said he was too busy to do it! I should add that it is the only piece of artwork that I have ever designed, since my main function in life is to write advertisements, prospectuses, magazine editorials etc and so on. You encourage me to try again . . .'

153 Book Token bookmarker (1973) printed in colour on thin white card with reproductions of the tokens designed for children. Length 15.4cm.
The reverse side shows the same tokens in black and white on a blue ground.

154 Bookmarker (1973) printed in green on a stiff mauve paper to mark the 600th performance given by the Scottish Opera on 11 December 1973. Length 17.2cm.
The reverse side is plain.

155 Bookmarker (1973) printed on thin card in black and white on a blue ground, to advertise Penguin books on natural history. Length 16.3cm.
The reverse side, printed in blue on a white ground, gives a selection of new books available in August 1973.

156 Folio Society bookmarker (1973–4) printed in black with a brown border, on card. Length 16cm.
The reverse side is identical.

153

Give the pleasure of choosing with Book Tokens

Puzzle inside

Dougal buys a book

ory inside

Picture to colour inside

154

Scottish Opera
December 11,
1973
Tonight's
performance
is the 600th
to be given by
Scottish Opera

155

ALL CREATURES GREAT AND SMALL...

Eugène Marais

THE SOUL OF THE APE 30p
THE SOUL OF THE WHITE ANT
30p

Victor B. Scheffer

THE YEAR OF THE SEAL 30p
THE YEAR OF THE WHALE 30p

From the social organization of a termite colony to the breeding habits of the sperm whale, these new Penguins take a scientific yet compassionate look at animals great and small, demanding sympathy and respect instead of our usual indifference and exploitation.

156

By far the largest number of advertising book-markers are now printed on strong glossy card and attached to the spines of reference books. They are made to last as long as the book is in use and the advertising is aimed at a particular group of people, usually professional and business groups. The Bishop & Sons marker (157), attached to *Debrett's Peerage*, is directed to property owners who might require a high-class removal and depository service. Here are some reference books with a note of the advertising carried on the bookmarkers attached to them:

The Municipal Year Book Francis Parker Building Services, and Thomas Fattorini Ltd, makers of badges of office, civic maces and insignia.

Crockfords Clerical Directory The Ecclesiastical Insurance Office Ltd.

The Hospitals Year Book Advertisements for hospital badges and the Isolette Infant Incubator.

The Directory of Directors Hambros Bank.

The Medical Practitioners' Year Book 'Ponderex, the leading treatment for overweight without amphetamine-like hazard'.

The Directory of Shipowners, Shipbuilders and Marine Engineers Weir Pumps Ltd.

The Trader Handbook for the Motor, Motor Cycle and Cycle Trades Bowater hire purchase and credit finance.

The list is endless, and each marker is clearly tailored to the potential readers. Such markers cannot be acquired for a collection until out-of-date copies have been discarded by the owners and the marker cords detached from the books. They are worth saving, nevertheless. In future years they will be of as much intrinsic interest as those with Victorian advertisements are today. Younger collectors especially would be foolish to pass by any interesting modern markers.

The Royal Air Force marker (158) not only seeks to recruit to the Service but also happily emphasises the true purpose of a bookmarker.

Most collections have their 'problem pieces'. Who, for example, published the bookmarker (159) which simply asks two questions: 'Have you forgotten the cork screw?' and 'Have you forgotten the salt?'? One of these bookmarkers has been found in a Nonesuch Press *Weekend Book* (1924), so perhaps it was printed as a reminder to weekenders?

Every collector will have his favourite book-marker. The author has a leather one issued by the King's Roll War Disabled Men's Association on which the following words are printed: 'Here I Fell Asleep'!

157 Bookmarker (1969) printed in black on thin glossy card with a gilt border to advertise the services offered by Bishop & Sons. The marker was attached to copies of 'Debrett's Peerage'. Length 22.8cm.

The reverse side gives a list of Bishop & Sons' warehouses.

158 Royal Air Force Recruiting bookmarker (1970s) printed in blue on thin blue card. This was issued by the Careers Information Centre, 23 Queen Victoria Street, Reading. Length 15.7cm.

159 Bookmarker with no clues to date or origin printed in black on buff paper. Length 20cm.

The reverse side is similar except for the question which is—'Have you forgotten the salt?'

157

The Founder

Bishop & Sons
Depositories Ltd

A
Heritage of Personal
Service
1854·1969

The fascinating story of the Bishop family business started in 1854, when 20 year old Joseph James Bishop, known as 'JJ', was inspired to set up on his own. Thus started an era of success through personal service and efficient administration. This is as true today as it was in 1854. Their many friends in the Trade will testify to the assistance and goodwill given by the Bishop family over many years. Although specialising in the carriage of part loads and small lots, there is no job too big or too small, which cannot be moved throughout the U.K., and abroad, by the Bishop's Move Group.

158

PLEASE

DO NOT MARK

YOUR PLACE

BY

TURNING DOWN

THE CORNER

OF A PAGE

———

USE THIS

159

*Have
you
forgotten
the
cork
screw?*

INDEX

(numbers refer to pages)